Eyebrow Microblading

Comprehensive Course in Dermopigmentation and Permanent Makeup

Indice

I. Introduction to Microblading and Eyebrow Dermopigmentation 15

1. What is Microblading 15
2. What is Eyebrow Dermopigmentation 16
3. Differences between Microblading and Dermopigmentation 18
4. Advantages and Limitations of Microblading and Dermopigmentation 19
5. Popularity and Demand for Microblading and Dermopigmentation 22

II. History and Evolution of Microblading and Permanent Makeup 25

1. Origins of Microblading: From Ancient Techniques to Modern Innovation 25
2. The Historical Journey of Permanent Makeup: From Early Applications to Advanced Techniques 26
3. Technological Transformations in Permanent Makeup: From Manual to Automated Techniques 28
4. Globalization of Microblading: How Local Cultures Contributed to its Spread 29
5. The Influence of Celebrities on the Evolution of Microblading and Permanent Make Up 31

III. Eyebrow Anatomy and Facial Structure 33

1. Eyebrow Structure: Analysis of Components and Anatomical Parts 33
2. The Relationship Between Eyebrows and Face: Harmony of Proportions and Expression 35

3. Types of Eyebrows Based on Face Shape: Morphological Adaptation and Personal Style......36

4. The Role of Eyebrows in Facial Expression: Nonverbal Communication and Emotion..............38

5. Aging Process and Eyebrows: Anatomical Changes and Corrective Treatments...............................39

IV. Tools and Materials Needed for Microblading and Dermopigmentation...41

1. Essential Tools for Microblading..............................41
2. Essential Materials for Dermopigmentation............42
3. Microblading: Precision Tools for Creating Fine Hair Strokes...44
4. Dermopigmentation: Pigments and Colors for a Natural Result..46
5. Auxiliary Tools for Workspace Preparation............47
6. Materials for Hygiene and Safety during Procedures 48
7. Accessories for Client Consultation and Facial Analysis..50
8. Specialized Tools for Corrections and Touch-Ups During the Process..51

V. Workspace Preparation and Hygiene Measures.....53

1. Surface Cleaning and Disinfection Procedure........53
2. Using Sterile Equipment During Preparation..........54
3. Organization and Arrangement of Tools on the Workstation..56
4. Hygiene Standards for the Aesthetician's Personal Cleanliness...57
5. Using Workstation Protections................................58
6. Biological Waste Disposal Procedures...................60

VI. Client Consultation and Facial Analysis..............63

1. Introduction to the Consultation: Welcoming the Client and Setting Expectations..........................63
2. Facial Morphological Analysis: Identifying Eyebrow Shape and Proportions..64
3. Assessing Client Desires: Active Listening and Effective Communication......................................65
4. Colorimetry Considerations: Choosing the Pigment Color Based on Skin Tone and Hair Color...........67
5. Defining the Work Plan: Determining the Shape and Style of the Eyebrows...68

VII. Colorimetry and Color Selection......................71

1. Principles of Colorimetry Applied to Microblading and Dermopigmentation..71
2. Assessing Skin Tone and Undertones for Color Selection..72
3. Using Color Wheels for Accurate Shade Selection 73
4. Adjusting Eyebrow Color to the Client's Individual Characteristics..75
5. Advanced Techniques for Eyebrow Color Customization..76
6. Considerations on Duration and Color Change Over Time..78

VIII. Eyebrow Drawing and Shaping Techniques......81

1. Introduction to Eyebrow Drawing Techniques........81
2. Morphological Assessment of the Client's Eyebrows 82
3. Identifying the Ideal Eyebrow Shape......................84
4. Pencil Drawing Techniques: Definition and Recommended Practices..85

5. Using Thread for Eyebrow Shaping: Procedures and Tips......86
6. Hair Removal Techniques: Waxing, Tweezing, and Alternative Methods......88
7. Application of Eyebrow Cosmetics: Pencils, Gels, and Powders......89
8. Eyebrow Tinting Techniques: Procedures and Considerations......90
9. Final Touches and Eyebrow Maintenance Tips......92

IX. Practice of Eyebrow Tracing with Pencils and Stencils......95

1. Introduction to Eyebrow Mapping......95
2. Using Pencils for Eyebrow Mapping......96
3. Eyebrow Mapping Techniques with Pencils......97
4. Choosing Eyebrow Stencils for Mapping......98
5. Eyebrow Mapping Procedure with Stencils......99
6. Correction and Refinement of Eyebrow Mapping.101
7. Practical Tips for Eyebrow Mapping with Pencils and Stencils......102

X. Local Anesthesia Techniques and Pain Management......105

1. Types of Local Anesthesia: Selection and Application......105
2. Pain Management in Microblading: Strategies and Protocols......106
3. Topical Anesthetics: Application and Waiting Times 108
4. Considerations for Anesthesia in Dermopigmentation: Risks and Benefits......109

    5. Approaches to Pain Reduction During Treatment: Tips and Advice..111

XI. Application of the Microblading Technique.......115

    1. Preparation of Tools and Workspace...................115
    2. Preliminary Eyebrow Design...............................116
    3. Choosing the Color and Shape of Microblading Blades...117
    4. Technique for Incision and Pigment Insertion......118
    5. Depth Control of Incisions..................................120
    6. Creating Realistic and Natural Lines...................121
    7. Managing Eyebrow Symmetry and Arch.............122
    8. Post-Treatment Application and Eyebrow Care Tips 123

XII. Application of Shading Technique for Fuller Eyebrows..125

    1. Introduction to the Shading Technique for Fuller Eyebrows...125
    2. Selection of Tools and Pigments for Eyebrow Shading...126
    3. Shading and Ombre Techniques for Fuller Eyebrows 128
    4. Step-by-Step Procedure for Applying Eyebrow Shading...129
    5. Managing Color and Shape During Eyebrow Shading Application..131
    6. Correction and Refinement of Eyebrows After Shading Application..133
    7. Post-Treatment Care Tips for Shaded Eyebrows.135
    8. Expected Results and Possible Risks Associated with the Shading Technique................................136

XIII. Corrections and Touch-ups in Microblading and Dermopigmentation 139

1. Touch-Up Procedures in Microblading and Dermopigmentation 139
2. Identifying Areas to Correct 140
3. Color Correction Techniques 142
4. Methods for Adjusting Eyebrow Shape 143
5. Managing Scars and Asymmetries 144
6. Tips for an Effective and Long-Lasting Touch-Up 145

XIV. Managing Clients with Scars or Dermatological Conditions 149

1. Assessment of Scars and Dermatological Conditions 149
2. Specialized Approaches for Scar Management ... 150
3. Considerations During the Pre-Treatment Consultation 151
4. Specific Techniques for Scars and Dermatological Conditions 152
5. Post-Treatment Care Tips for Clients with Scars or Dermatological Conditions 154

XV. Precautions and Safety in Performing Procedures 157

1. Use of Personal Protective Equipment (PPE) 157
2. Sterilization and Disinfection of Tools 158
3. Work Environment Control 159
4. Prevention of Adverse Skin Reactions 161
5. Emergency Management During Procedures 162

XVI. Marketing and Promotion of Microblading and Dermopigmentation Services..................165

1. Online Marketing Strategies...............165
2. Collaborations with Influencers and Industry Professionals..........................167
3. Using Social Media to Promote Services..............168
4. Industry Events and Trade Shows: Promotional Opportunities..........................169

XVII. Equipment Management and Material Procurement..................171

1. Equipment Selection: Choosing the Right Tool for Each Procedure....................171
2. Maintenance and Cleaning of Equipment: Ensuring Safety and Longevity........................172
3. Sourcing Materials: Strategies for Obtaining Quality Products..........................173
4. Quality Control: Verification and Testing of Purchased Materials........................175
5. Workspace Organization: Optimizing for Maximum Efficiency..........................176
6. Storage and Preservation: Maintaining Material Integrity Over Time........................177
7. Inventory Monitoring: Avoiding Stockouts and Ensuring Operational Continuity..................179
8. Sustainability and Waste Reduction: Eco-Friendly Practices for Managing Equipment and Materials 181

XVIII. Legal and Regulatory Aspects of Microblading and Dermopigmentation Practice..................183

1. Legislation on Cosmetic Practices: Regulations and Legal Requirements... 183
2. Training and Certification Requirements for Industry Professionals.. 185
3. Legal and Insurance Responsibilities for Microblading and Dermopigmentation Practitioners 186
4. Health and Safety Regulations to Ensure Client Safety.. 188
5. Documentation and Informed Consent: Role and Importance in Aesthetic Treatments.................. 189

XIX. Troubleshooting and Managing Challenges During Procedures.. 191

1. Identifying Issues During Procedures................... 191
2. Real-Time Problem-Solving Strategies................. 192
3. Managing Post-Treatment Complications............. 194
4. Effective Communication with Clients During Issues 196
5. Continuous Improvement of Work Processes...... 197

XX. Professional Development and Skill Advancement in Microblading and Permanent Makeup................... 199

1. Advanced Training Programs and Specializations 199
2. Continuing Education Courses and Hands-On Workshops... 200
3. Advanced Microblading Techniques Mastery........ 201
4. Exploring New Technologies in Permanent Makeup 202
5. Certification Paths and Professional Recognition. 203

🎁 **At the end of this book you'll find an exclusive gift!**

Eyebrow Microblading

Comprehensive Course in Dermopigmentation and Permanent Makeup

I. Introduction to Microblading and Eyebrow Dermopigmentation

1. What is Microblading

Microblading is an innovative and increasingly popular beauty technique for achieving well-defined and natural-looking eyebrows. This semi-permanent procedure involves the use of ultra-thin microblades to deposit pigment beneath the skin, creating hair-like strokes that mimic real eyebrow hairs. Thanks to the precision and versatility of this technique, it is possible to correct irregular shapes, increase eyebrow density, and enhance the overall appearance of the face. The final result is a flawless and long-lasting look, eliminating the need for daily eyebrow makeup.

The microblading process begins with a detailed consultation with the client, during which aesthetic preferences and desired outcomes are discussed. This step is crucial for understanding the client's expectations and customizing the procedure accordingly. After the consultation, a thorough facial analysis is conducted, assessing the existing eyebrow shape, facial symmetry, and other relevant features.

Once the analysis is complete, the colorimetry and color selection phase begins. It is important to choose a color that matches the client's natural eyebrow tone and blends harmoniously with their face. During this phase, the specialized esthetician uses their expertise to determine the most suitable color, considering various factors such as skin tone, hair color, and the client's personal preferences.

With the color selected, the drawing and shaping of the eyebrows proceed. Using specially designed pencils and stencils, the esthetician outlines the desired eyebrow shape, following the facial structure and ensuring perfect symmetry. This step is crucial for achieving a harmonious and natural final result, enhancing the client's facial features.

Once the drawing is complete, the main phase of the microblading procedure begins: the pigment application. Using the microblades, the esthetician creates precise and controlled strokes beneath the skin, mimicking the natural growth of eyebrow hairs. This process requires great skill and attention to detail, ensuring the pigment is evenly distributed and the final result is impeccable.

Finally, after the pigment application is complete, touch-ups and corrections are made to ensure a perfect finish. This may include adjusting the eyebrow shape or modifying the color to achieve the desired result. Once the procedure is finished, the client can enjoy perfectly defined eyebrows for months, minimizing the need for daily touch-ups.

2. What is Eyebrow Dermopigmentation

Eyebrow dermopigmentation, also known as permanent makeup, is an advanced technique in the field of aesthetics that aims to enhance the appearance of eyebrows through the application of permanent pigments. This procedure offers a long-lasting solution for coloring and defining eyebrows, eliminating the need for daily makeup application to achieve the desired look.

Unlike microblading, which uses microblades to create hair-like strokes, dermopigmentation involves the use of specialized tools, such as single or multiple-needle machines, to deposit pigment into deeper layers of the skin. This process allows for a more uniform and complete coverage of the eyebrows, ideal for coloring and defining even the sparsest or hairless areas.

Eyebrow dermopigmentation is particularly suitable for those who seek a long-term solution to improve the shape and color of their eyebrows. This technique can be used to fill in sparse eyebrows, correct asymmetries, or simply add definition and intensity to the face.

During the dermopigmentation procedure, the specialized esthetician uses their experience and knowledge of colorimetry to select the most suitable color for the client's needs. It is important to consider the skin tone, hair color, and the client's personal preferences to ensure a natural and harmonious result.

Once the procedure is complete, the newly pigmented eyebrows may appear darker than the final color. This is normal and due to the healing phase of the skin, during which the pigment will stabilize and adjust to the desired tone. It is important to follow the post-treatment instructions provided by the esthetician carefully to ensure optimal healing and a satisfactory final result.

In conclusion, eyebrow dermopigmentation is a versatile and reliable technique for achieving well-defined and long-lasting eyebrows. With proper preparation and attention to detail, it is possible to achieve remarkable results that enhance the natural beauty and appearance of each client.

3. Differences between Microblading and Dermopigmentation

While microblading and eyebrow dermopigmentation share similar goals, there are fundamental differences between the two techniques that are important to understand before choosing the procedure that best suits your needs.

Firstly, one of the main differences lies in the process itself. Microblading involves the use of ultra-thin microblades to create hair-like strokes, depositing pigment beneath the skin. This technique is ideal for creating a "hair-by-hair" effect and achieving the most natural-looking eyebrows possible. On the other hand, dermopigmentation uses single or multiple-needle machines to deposit pigment deeper into the skin, providing a more uniform and complete coverage of the eyebrows.

Another significant difference concerns the longevity of the results. Microblading is considered a semi-permanent technique, as the pigment tends to fade over time due to the natural turnover of skin cells. Typically, microblading can last from 1 to 3 years, depending on the client's skin type and environmental factors. In contrast, dermopigmentation is considered more permanent since the pigment is deposited deeper into the skin and tends to last longer. However, dermopigmentation pigment can also gradually fade over the years, requiring occasional touch-ups to maintain the desired result.

Additionally, the two techniques differ in the type of pigment used. In microblading, specific pigments are formulated to adhere to the skin and maintain their vibrancy over time. These pigments are often lighter and finer compared to the pigments used in dermopigmentation, which are designed for greater durability and resistance to fading over time.

Finally, it is important to consider the healing times and potential discomfort associated with each technique. Since microblading involves the use of thinner blades and shallower strokes, the healing time tends to be quicker and the discomfort during the procedure is generally less compared to dermopigmentation, which may require a longer healing time and cause a higher level of discomfort during and after treatment.

In conclusion, both microblading and eyebrow dermopigmentation are effective techniques for enhancing the appearance of eyebrows and achieving long-lasting results. However, it is important to understand the differences between the two techniques and consult with a qualified professional to determine which is the best choice for your aesthetic needs.

4. Advantages and Limitations of Microblading and Dermopigmentation

Both microblading and eyebrow dermopigmentation offer a range of unique advantages, but it is also important to be aware of the potential limitations associated with each technique. Let's take a closer look at the pros and cons of both treatments to help you make an informed decision.

Advantages of Microblading:

Natural Appearance: One of the main advantages of microblading is its ability to create natural-looking eyebrows. Thanks to the precision of the microblades, it is possible to mimic the natural growth of eyebrow hairs, achieving an aesthetically pleasing and realistic result.

Semi-Permanence: Microblading offers a semi-permanent solution to enhance the appearance of the eyebrows. While the pigment tends to fade over time, the duration of the procedure allows clients to enjoy well-defined eyebrows for several years without the need for frequent touch-ups.

Flexibility and Customization: Microblading allows for a high degree of flexibility and customization. The specialized esthetician can adapt the shape, color, and density of the eyebrows based on the client's individual preferences, ensuring tailored and satisfactory results.

Quick Healing Time: Since microblading involves superficial strokes under the skin, the healing time is generally quick. Clients can return to their daily activities soon after the procedure without significant interruptions.

Limitations of Microblading:

Limited Longevity: Despite its semi-permanence, microblading has limited longevity. The pigment tends to fade over the months or initial years, requiring touch-ups to maintain the desired result.

Availability of Qualified Professionals: Since microblading requires a skilled hand and a thorough knowledge of eyebrow anatomy, it can be challenging to find qualified and reliable professionals in some geographic areas.

High Initial Cost: The initial cost of microblading can be significant, especially when considering the need for future touch-ups. However, many clients find that the long-term value of the results justifies the initial expense.

Advantages of Dermopigmentation:

Prolonged Duration: One of the main advantages of dermopigmentation is its longer-lasting results compared to microblading. The pigment deposited deeper into the skin tends to last longer, offering durable results with minimal need for touch-ups.

Complete Coverage: Dermopigmentation provides more complete coverage of the eyebrows, ideal for coloring and defining even the sparsest or hairless areas.

Suitable for Oily or Combination Skin: Since the pigment is deposited deeper into the skin, dermopigmentation is often a better choice for those with oily or combination skin, who may find microblading less long-lasting.

Wide Range of Colors: Dermopigmentation offers a wide range of colors to choose from, allowing for greater customization and adaptability to the client's needs.

Limitations of Dermopigmentation:

Less Natural Appearance: Due to the deeper pigment deposition, dermopigmentation may result in a less natural appearance compared to microblading, especially if not performed by an experienced professional.

Prolonged Healing Time: Since dermopigmentation involves deeper pigment penetration, the healing time tends to be longer compared to microblading, with potential swelling and redness post-treatment that may take a few days to fully resolve.

In conclusion, both microblading and eyebrow dermopigmentation offer a range of unique advantages and limitations. It is important to consult with a qualified professional to determine which technique is best suited to your needs and aesthetic preferences.

5. Popularity and Demand for Microblading and Dermopigmentation

The rise of microblading and eyebrow dermopigmentation in recent years has marked a significant transformation in the aesthetics industry. The growing popularity of these techniques reflects an increasing demand from consumers who desire impeccable, well-defined eyebrows without the hassle of daily makeup. This section will explore the reasons behind their rising popularity and the ongoing enthusiasm for these procedures.

Microblading:

Aesthetic and Cosmetic Appeal: Microblading has gained widespread popularity due to its ability to create natural and flawless-looking eyebrows. With the growing focus on aesthetic trends and celebrities flaunting perfect brows, more people are seeking ways to achieve the same look in a durable and convenient manner.

Technological Innovation: The advent of new technologies and materials in the aesthetics industry has made microblading safer, more precise, and more effective than ever before. Improvements in pigments and tools have made this procedure more accessible and reliable for a wider range of clients.

Dermopigmentation:

Long-Term Solution: Dermopigmentation offers a long-term solution for coloring and defining eyebrows, appealing to those who seek lasting results without the need for frequent touch-ups. This technique has gained popularity among those who want to save time and effort in their daily makeup routine.

Versatility in Applications: Beyond eyebrows, dermopigmentation can be used to enhance various facial features, such as lips and eyes. This versatility has broadened its appeal among individuals looking for a comprehensive way to enhance their overall appearance.

Ongoing Demand:

Evolving Beauty Trends: With the ever-changing beauty trends and the increasing focus on personal appearance, the demand for microblading and dermopigmentation continues to grow. Clients are constantly looking for new ways to enhance and perfect their looks, driving the demand for these innovative procedures.

Word-of-Mouth and Recommendations: The success of microblading and dermopigmentation is also fueled by the power of word-of-mouth and recommendations. Satisfied clients enthusiastically share their results with friends and family, helping to spread awareness and increase demand for these techniques.

In conclusion, the growing popularity of microblading and eyebrow dermopigmentation results from a combination of aesthetic, technological, and social factors. These techniques continue to generate interest and excitement among consumers, promising perfect eyebrows and a flawless appearance for years to come.

II. History and Evolution of Microblading and Permanent Makeup

1. Origins of Microblading: From Ancient Techniques to Modern Innovation

Microblading, though now considered a cutting-edge technique in eyebrow aesthetics, has ancient roots dating back centuries. This paragraph will explore the historical origins of microblading, tracing its evolutionary path from traditional techniques to modern innovations.

The earliest traces of microblading can be found in ancient cultures such as Japan and China. In Japan, for instance, there was a practice known as "Kumadori," which involved using charcoal powders to draw fine, defined lines on the face, including the eyebrows. This technique was primarily used in theatrical arts to emphasize performers' facial expressions and convey emotions to the audience.

Similarly, in China, the practice of microblading was widespread among rural populations, where women used rudimentary tools like bamboo sticks and natural pigments to create hair-like strokes on their eyebrows. This technique was often associated with cultural rituals and wedding ceremonies, where defined eyebrows symbolized beauty and fertility.

Over the centuries, microblading underwent various transformations and adaptations across different cultures worldwide. However, it was only in the modern era that this technique experienced a true revolution thanks to technological innovation and scientific research.

With the advent of modern technology and the evolution of materials and tools, microblading has achieved levels of precision and refinement never seen before. The introduction of ultra-thin micro blades and specially formulated pigments has enabled aestheticians to create incredibly realistic and well-defined eyebrows, meeting the aesthetic demands of even the most discerning clients.

In conclusion, the origins of microblading lie in ancient cultural practices that have stood the test of time and evolved into the advanced and sophisticated technique we know today. This historical journey offers a valuable perspective on the significance and impact of microblading in contemporary aesthetics.

2. The Historical Journey of Permanent Makeup: From Early Applications to Advanced Techniques

The concept of permanent makeup, also known as permanent or semi-permanent makeup, dates back thousands of years when ancient civilizations used natural pigments to decorate and enhance facial features. However, it is only in the past century that this practice has truly evolved, transitioning from rudimentary early applications to the advanced and sophisticated techniques that characterize modern aesthetics.

The earliest forms of permanent makeup emerged in the 1920s when women began using permanent tattoos to define their eyebrows and outline their lips. These initial applications, although effective in creating a more defined and harmonious appearance, were often limited by the technology and materials available at the time. The pigments used were generally more limited in terms of color and longevity, and the procedures could be painful and risky due to the lack of advanced tools and techniques.

In the following years, with the advancement of technology and the growing popularity of permanent makeup, new techniques and approaches emerged to improve the practice. Aestheticians began using specialized machines and tools designed specifically for permanent makeup, allowing for greater precision and control during procedures. Pigments became more advanced and long-lasting, ensuring more consistent and reliable results over time.

In recent decades, permanent makeup has undergone further innovations and improvements thanks to ongoing research and development in the aesthetics industry. New techniques, such as digital dermopigmentation, have made permanent makeup even more precise and effective, enabling aestheticians to create stunning results with minimal discomfort for the client. Laser technology has also revolutionized the process of removing permanent makeup, offering a safe and effective option for those who wish to eliminate or correct unwanted pigments.

In conclusion, the historical journey of permanent makeup represents a continuous evolution from antiquity to the present day. This practice has gone through many stages of development and improvement, culminating in advanced and sophisticated techniques that offer stunning and long-lasting results for clients seeking beauty and aesthetic perfection.

3. Technological Transformations in Permanent Makeup: From Manual to Automated Techniques

Technological transformations in the field of permanent makeup have radically revolutionized the approach and practice of this cosmetic art form. Once requiring a high degree of manual skill and craftsmanship, permanent makeup is now supported by a wide range of advanced technologies that enhance the efficiency, precision, and safety of procedures.

One of the main technological advancements in permanent makeup has been the introduction of automated machines designed specifically to perform dermopigmentation procedures more quickly and accurately than the human hand. These devices use sterile, precise needles controlled by computers, which can penetrate the dermis evenly to deposit pigments with millimeter precision. This automation not only reduces the time required to complete a procedure but also minimizes the margin of human error, ensuring more consistent and satisfactory results.

In addition to automated application technology, there are also advanced tools used for the preparation and analysis of the treatment areas. High-resolution digital cameras allow aestheticians to capture detailed images of the client's facial features, enabling precise assessment of eyebrow symmetry and shape before the procedure. These images can also be used to digitally simulate the desired results, allowing the client to visualize and approve the expected outcome before the treatment begins.

Moreover, the pigments used in permanent makeup have undergone significant improvements thanks to advancements in cosmetic technology. Modern pigments are formulated to be more stable over time and less susceptible to fading, ensuring long-lasting and consistent results over the years. Additionally, these pigments are often hypoallergenic and clinically tested to minimize the risk of adverse reactions for the client.

In conclusion, technological transformations in the field of permanent makeup have ushered in a new era of precision, safety, and efficiency in dermopigmentation procedures. These innovations continue to enhance the client experience and elevate professional standards in the cosmetic aesthetics industry.

4. Globalization of Microblading: How Local Cultures Contributed to its Spread

Microblading, a once geographically confined eyebrow beauty technique, has experienced global diffusion in recent decades. This expansion has been driven by various factors, including globalization, information accessibility, and a growing interest in personalized aesthetics.

One of the primary drivers of microblading's globalization has been the ability to share and disseminate information through the Internet and social media. Platforms like Instagram, YouTube, and Facebook have allowed microblading artists to showcase their work to an international audience, highlighting their impressive results and attracting the interest of potential clients worldwide. This online visibility has significantly contributed to making microblading a well-known and sought-after practice beyond its cultural origins.

Additionally, globalization has opened up new opportunities for training and learning in the field of microblading. Training courses and certifications have become internationally accessible, enabling aspiring microblading artists to acquire skills and knowledge even outside the countries where the practice is traditionally rooted. This has helped create a global community of microblading professionals who share experiences, techniques, and innovations to continuously improve the quality of their results.

Furthermore, the spread of microblading has also been facilitated by cultural and aesthetic influences. Many countries have embraced the concept of well-defined and well-groomed eyebrows, thereby driving the spread of microblading across the globe. For instance, in South Korea, the concept of "eyebrow embroidery" has become extremely popular, leading to a growing demand for microblading services not only within the country but also abroad, as Korean beauty trends have influenced popular culture worldwide.

In summary, the globalization of microblading has been a complex phenomenon fueled by a combination of cultural, technological, and economic factors. This diffusion has opened new opportunities for microblading artists and allowed more people to access this innovative and transformative practice to enhance their appearance and self-esteem.

5. The Influence of Celebrities on the Evolution of Microblading and Permanent Make Up

Celebrities have always wielded significant influence over beauty trends and cosmetic practices, and microblading and permanent make up are no exception. In recent years, many celebrities have publicly shared their experiences with these procedures, thereby helping to raise awareness and acceptance of these practices among the general public.

The influence of celebrities on microblading and permanent make up can be observed in several ways. Firstly, many celebrities have openly shared their journey with these procedures through social media and public interviews. Through before-and-after photos, video tutorials, and personal accounts, they have showcased the impressive results and transformation that microblading and permanent make up can bring to their eyebrows and overall appearance. This has helped demystify the procedures and break down taboos associated with permanent makeup, making it more acceptable and desirable for the general audience.

Moreover, many celebrities have actively played a role in promoting and endorsing brands and clinics specializing in microblading and permanent make up. Through collaborations with cosmetic brands and world-renowned estheticians, they have helped to familiarize these practices to a broader audience and advocate for higher professional standards in the industry. This media exposure has increased the visibility and credibility of microblading and permanent make up as viable options for enhancing appearance and self-confidence.

Additionally, we cannot ignore the impact that the iconic eyebrows of some celebrities have had on popular aesthetics and beauty trends. Celebrities like Cara Delevingne, Kim Kardashian, and Rihanna have contributed to making thick and defined eyebrows a symbol of beauty and style. This has prompted many people to seek ways to achieve the same look, thereby increasing the demand for procedures such as microblading and permanent make up.

In conclusion, the influence of celebrities on the evolution of microblading and permanent make up has been significant and enduring. Through their media visibility, personal testimonials, and impact on beauty trends, celebrities have played a crucial role in making these practices more accessible, acceptable, and desirable for the general public.

III. Eyebrow Anatomy and Facial Structure

1. Eyebrow Structure: Analysis of Components and Anatomical Parts

To fully understand the process of shaping and enhancing eyebrows through techniques like microblading and dermopigmentation, it's essential to have a detailed knowledge of the anatomical structure of the eyebrows themselves. Eyebrows are not merely strands of hair adorning the brow ridge; they are complex structures that serve a range of important physiological and aesthetic functions within the context of the human face.

In order to analyze the structure of eyebrows comprehensively, it's useful to break them down into different components and anatomical parts. First and foremost, let's examine the brow arch area, which is the most prominent part of the eyebrows and significantly contributes to the overall facial expression. This region is characterized by a natural curvature that varies from individual to individual and can be shaped and enhanced through microblading and dermopigmentation techniques to achieve a more defined and harmonious arch.

In addition to the brow arch, another important component of the eyebrows is the brow body area, which extends laterally from the arch and follows the upper contour of the eye socket. This part of the eyebrows can vary in thickness and density depending on genetics and individual facial characteristics. In microblading and dermopigmentation, it's crucial to consider the shape and length of the brow body to achieve balanced and natural aesthetic results.

Lastly, we need to examine the tail of the eyebrows, which is the end part of the eyebrows located at the lateral edge of the arch. The shape and length of the eyebrow tail can significantly influence the overall appearance of the face and its symmetry. Techniques like microblading can be used to correct any asymmetries in the shape or length of the eyebrow tail, ensuring a more balanced and harmonious look.

In conclusion, analyzing the components and anatomical parts of eyebrows provides an essential foundation for effectively performing aesthetic enhancement techniques such as microblading and dermopigmentation. Understanding the structure of eyebrows allows estheticians to assess the individual facial features of the client and create customized results that enhance aesthetic appearance and self-confidence.

2. The Relationship Between Eyebrows and Face: Harmony of Proportions and Expression

Eyebrows play a fundamental role in the harmony of proportions of the human face and in a person's emotional expression. Their shape, size, and position directly influence the overall appearance of the face and the ability to communicate emotions through facial expressions. Therefore, understanding and respecting the relationship between eyebrows and the face is crucial for achieving satisfying and natural aesthetic results through techniques such as microblading and dermopigmentation.

Firstly, it's important to consider the shape of the face when shaping eyebrows. Facial proportions can vary significantly from individual to individual and include shapes such as oval, round, square, and heart-shaped. The face shape will influence the choice of eyebrow shape and architecture, aiming to create a harmonious balance between the facial features and the eyebrows themselves. For example, for a round face, opting for eyebrows with a slightly angular shape may be advisable to create an elongating and slimming effect, while for an oval face, fuller and rounded eyebrows can help balance the proportions.

In addition to the face shape, it's crucial to consider the position of the eyebrows in relation to the eyes and other facial features. Well-positioned eyebrows can open up the gaze, define the eyelid crease, and enhance the overall appearance of the face. However, incorrect eyebrow positioning can have the opposite effect, creating a tired, sad, or angry appearance. Therefore, during microblading and dermopigmentation procedures, careful evaluation of eyebrow position is essential, and adjustments may be necessary to ensure an optimal aesthetic outcome.

Lastly, the color and shade of the eyebrows in relation to hair and skin color should also be considered. Eyebrow color should harmonize with the rest of the facial features and enhance the client's natural beauty. During microblading and dermopigmentation procedures, specially formulated pigments can be selected to match the client's hair and skin color, ensuring a natural and flawless result.

In conclusion, the relationship between eyebrows and the face is a key element to consider during the process of shaping and enhancing eyebrows. Respecting the harmony of proportions and expression of the face allows estheticians to create customized aesthetic results that enhance the overall appearance of the client and accentuate their natural beauty.

3. Types of Eyebrows Based on Face Shape: Morphological Adaptation and Personal Style

Different face shapes require distinct approaches in eyebrow shaping to accentuate distinctive features and create a balanced, harmonious appearance. Therefore, it is crucial to understand the specific characteristics of each face shape and adapt the eyebrows accordingly to achieve optimal aesthetic results. Let's explore the types of eyebrows most suitable for various face shapes and how these can be personalized to reflect the client's individual style and preferences.

For oval faces, characterized by slightly greater length than width and soft, rounded lines, slightly arched and fairly full eyebrows can complement the natural and harmonious appearance of the face. The gently arched shape helps create a sense of elongation and slimness, while the density of the eyebrows helps balance the overall face structure.

In the case of round faces, characterized by soft, curved lines without pronounced angles, it is advisable to opt for slightly angular eyebrows to create an elongating and slimming effect. Eyebrows with a more defined arch and a shape slightly tilted upwards can contribute to giving a sense of verticality to the face and balance the overall proportions.

For square faces, which have sharp lines and pronounced angles, softer and rounded eyebrows can help soften the stiffness of the face lines. Slightly rounded and not too thin eyebrows can contribute to a softer and more feminine appearance to the square face, creating a pleasant contrast with the sharper lines of the jaw and cheeks.

Finally, for heart-shaped faces, characterized by a broad forehead and a narrower jawline, fuller and well-defined eyebrows can help balance the proportions of the face. Eyebrows with a natural shape and a slight curvature can help create a balanced effect between the broader forehead and the narrower jawline, enhancing the overall appearance of the face.

In summary, adapting eyebrows to the face shape is essential for achieving harmonious and satisfying aesthetic results. Understanding the specific characteristics of each face shape and selecting the most suitable eyebrows can make a difference in the overall appearance of the client, enhancing their self-esteem and confidence.

4. The Role of Eyebrows in Facial Expression: Nonverbal Communication and Emotion

Eyebrows play a fundamental role in nonverbal communication and the emotional expression of the human face. Beyond their aesthetic function of defining the face's appearance, eyebrows are essential for conveying a wide range of emotions and moods through subtle movements and variations in their shape and position. This critical role of eyebrows in facial expression has been extensively studied in the fields of psychology and nonverbal communication. Understanding how eyebrows influence the perception and interpretation of emotions can be valuable for aestheticians aiming to create aesthetic results that reflect the authenticity and naturalness of human expressions.

Eyebrows can take on a variety of shapes and positions that communicate different emotions. For instance, raised eyebrows can indicate surprise or interest, while furrowed brows may suggest concern or disapproval. Additionally, the shape and curvature of eyebrows can influence the overall appearance of the face and contribute to creating an atmosphere of kindness, severity, or trust, depending on individual preferences and social context.

Moreover, eyebrows play a crucial role in communicating sympathy and empathy. Slightly raised or arched eyebrows can suggest interest and openness towards others, whereas lowered eyebrows may convey disinterest or distrust. Aestheticians must therefore carefully consider the shape and position of eyebrows during shaping and enhancement procedures to create a welcoming and reassuring atmosphere that facilitates effective communication and emotional connection with the client.

Furthermore, it is important to recognize that eyebrows can vary significantly from person to person in terms of density, color, and natural shape. This individual diversity can influence the perception and interpretation of emotions through eyebrows, necessitating a personalized approach in eyebrow shaping and enhancement to ensure authentic aesthetic results that respect the client's unique characteristics.

In summary, the role of eyebrows in facial expression is crucial for nonverbal communication and the emotional expression of the human face. Understanding how eyebrows influence the perception and interpretation of emotions can help aestheticians create aesthetic results that reflect the authenticity and naturalness of human expressions, thereby enhancing the overall appearance of the client and their emotional connection with the surrounding world.

5. Aging Process and Eyebrows: Anatomical Changes and Corrective Treatments

As time passes, the face undergoes a series of anatomical changes that also affect the shape and appearance of the eyebrows. The aging process leads to a decrease in collagen and elastin production, which can cause a loss of skin tone and elasticity, including the sagging of the forehead and eyebrows. These changes can result in a lower position of the eyebrows compared to their youthful natural position, creating a more tired, drooping, or angry appearance.

Additionally, aging can also bring changes in the density and pigmentation of eyebrow hair. Many people experience a reduction in eyebrow hair density, which can make the eyebrows thinner and less defined. At the same time, eyebrow hair can turn gray or white, contributing to an overall appearance of aging and loss of vitality.

To address these aging-related changes in the eyebrows, there are several corrective treatments available, including microblading and dermopigmentation. These techniques allow aestheticians to redesign and enhance the shape, density, and color of the eyebrows, creating a younger, fresher, and more vibrant appearance. Through microblading, precise, thin hair strokes can be manually added to the eyebrow area, replicating the natural look of hair and enhancing definition and shape. On the other hand, dermopigmentation offers the option to add pigment to the skin of the eyebrows, creating a filling and defining effect that lasts over time.

However, it is important to consider that corrective treatments for aging-related eyebrow issues should be performed carefully and skillfully by qualified professionals. The skin on the face, including the eyebrow area, can become thinner and more sensitive with age, so it is essential to use safe and approved techniques to minimize the risk of complications or skin damage. Aestheticians must also take into account the individual preferences of the client and work closely with them to ensure satisfactory and natural results.

In conclusion, the aging process can significantly influence the shape and appearance of the eyebrows, but through corrective treatments such as microblading and dermopigmentation, it is possible to improve and revitalize the eyebrows, creating a younger and fresher appearance. However, these treatments should be performed with caution and expertise by qualified professionals to ensure safe and satisfactory results for the client.

IV. Tools and Materials Needed for Microblading and Dermopigmentation

1. Essential Tools for Microblading

Microblading is an art that requires precision and specialized tools to achieve impeccable and long-lasting results. Before undertaking any microblading procedure, it is essential to familiarize oneself with a range of high-quality tools that are indispensable for performing the technique safely and effectively. These tools not only facilitate the creation of fine, detailed lines that mimic natural hair but also ensure hygiene and safety management throughout the entire process.

First and foremost, one of the fundamental tools for microblading is the microblading pen. This tool is designed with an ultra-thin blade-shaped blade that allows aestheticians to manually draw fine and precise hair strokes in the eyebrow area. Choosing a high-quality microblading pen is crucial, as a well-designed and sharp blade ensures greater precision and control during the procedure, minimizing the risk of skin injury or undesired outcomes.

In addition to the microblading pen, another essential tool is the microblading blade, which is the interchangeable part of the pen that holds the blade. Microblading blades come in a variety of sizes and shapes to suit the specific requirements of the procedure and the client. The choice of the right blade depends on the client's natural hair density, desired eyebrow shape, and the microblading technique preferred by the aesthetician.

To ensure precision and hygiene during the procedure, it is also important to use auxiliary tools such as a microblading ruler and caliper. These tools allow aestheticians to accurately measure eyebrow proportions, trace guidelines, and ensure symmetry and balance in the final appearance of the eyebrows. Moreover, using measuring tools reduces the risk of errors during the process and ensures consistent and uniform results for each client.

Finally, sterility and hygiene are of paramount importance in microblading, so it is essential to have tools for workspace preparation and instrument disinfection. These may include skin disinfectants, disposable gloves, face masks, and tools for instrument sterilization such as autoclaves or ultraviolet ray devices. Ensuring that all tools are clean and sterilized reduces the risk of infections or adverse reactions from the client, ensuring a safe and comfortable experience during the microblading procedure.

2. Essential Materials for Dermopigmentation

Dermopigmentation is a complex procedure that requires the use of various materials to ensure long-lasting and satisfactory results. Choosing the right materials is crucial for achieving uniform, safe, and durable pigmentations, as well as ensuring maximum hygiene and safety during the procedure. In this paragraph, we will examine the fundamental materials necessary to perform dermopigmentation effectively and professionally.

First and foremost, one of the most important materials for dermopigmentation is pigment. Pigments are coloring substances that are inserted into the upper layer of the skin to create the desired effect on the eyebrows. It is essential to choose high-quality pigments that are safe, stable over time, and matched to the client's natural skin and hair tone. Pigments must comply with safety standards and be approved by competent authorities to ensure the client's health and well-being.

In addition to pigments, another essential material for dermopigmentation is the micro-pigmentation needle. Micro-pigmentation needles are designed to gently penetrate the superficial layer of the skin and deposit pigment evenly and controlled. The choice of the right needle depends on the aesthetician's individual preferences, the dermopigmentation technique used, and the client's skin characteristics. Needles must be single-use and sterile to ensure maximum safety and minimize the risk of contamination or infection.

Another indispensable material is the pigmentation device, commonly known as a dermopigmentation machine or dermograph. This device is designed to hold the needles and control the speed and depth of penetration into the skin during the dermopigmentation procedure. It is important to choose a high-quality pigmentation device that is reliable, precise, and easy to use, to ensure consistent and satisfactory results for every client.

Finally, it is important to consider auxiliary materials necessary for preparing the workspace and ensuring maximum hygiene and safety during the procedure. These may include sterile gauze, skin disinfectants, disposable gloves, and face protection. Ensuring the use of clean and sterile materials reduces the risk of complications or adverse reactions during dermopigmentation, ensuring a safe and comfortable experience for the client.

3. Microblading: Precision Tools for Creating Fine Hair Strokes

Microblading is a precision technique that requires the use of specially designed tools to create fine and detailed hair strokes that mimic the natural appearance of eyebrow hairs. The tools used in microblading are essential for achieving realistic and long-lasting results that meet the client's expectations and enhance the overall aesthetic of the eyebrows.

One of the primary tools used in microblading is the microblading pen. This tool is designed with an ultra-thin and precise blade that allows estheticians to create thin and well-defined hair lines with extreme accuracy. The blade of the microblading pen is made of high-quality titanium alloy or stainless steel, and it is available in a variety of sizes and shapes to suit the individual preferences of the esthetician and the morphology of the client's eyebrows.

In addition to the microblading pen, another fundamental tool is the microblading pigment. Pigment is a special color designed to be inserted into the superficial layer of the skin during the microblading procedure. Choosing the right pigment is crucial to achieve a natural and long-lasting color that matches the client's skin and hair tone. Microblading pigments come in a wide range of shades and hues, and estheticians must be able to select the most suitable color to achieve optimal results.

Another crucial tool in the microblading process is the microblading blade, which is the interchangeable part of the pen that holds the blade. Microblading blades are available in various configurations, including U-shape, L-shape, and flexible U-shape, each designed to create different hair effects and adapt to the client's preferences. Choosing the right blade depends on the density and natural structure of the client's hair, as well as the desired outcome.

Furthermore, to ensure precision and symmetry during the microblading procedure, estheticians often use auxiliary tools such as microblading rulers and eyebrow stencils. These tools allow estheticians to trace guidelines and drawing patterns before starting the procedure, ensuring consistent and harmonious results for every client. Using precision tools during microblading is essential to ensure satisfying and long-lasting results that reflect the natural appearance of the eyebrows.

4. Dermopigmentation: Pigments and Colors for a Natural Result

Dermopigmentation, or permanent makeup, involves the application of pigments into the skin to enhance or correct the shape, color, and definition of eyebrows. The choice of pigments is crucial to achieve a natural and harmonious result that blends seamlessly with the client's face and skin tone.

When selecting pigments for eyebrow dermopigmentation, it's important to consider several factors including the client's natural hair and skin color, skin tone and undertone, as well as the client's personal preference. Dermopigmentation pigments come in a wide range of colors and shades, from warm tones to cool tones, from natural browns to deep blacks, from bright blondes to subtle grays. Estheticians must be able to choose the right color and shade to create a natural and customized result for each client.

In addition to color, the consistency and quality of the pigment are crucial factors to consider. Dermopigmentation pigments should be formulated to be stable over time and not fade or change color over time. It is important to use high-quality pigments that comply with safety standards and are approved by competent authorities to ensure the client's health and well-being.

During the dermopigmentation procedure, estheticians can mix different pigments to achieve the perfect color that suits the client's natural skin tone. This color blending technique allows estheticians to customize the result according to the client's preferences and create a natural and realistic appearance that harmonizes with the facial features.

Furthermore, estheticians must consider the skin healing process and how the pigment color may evolve over time. During the healing period, the pigment color may undergo slight variation and become softer and more natural. It is important to inform the client about what to expect during the healing process and provide detailed instructions on how to care for the eyebrows to ensure optimal results.

5. Auxiliary Tools for Workspace Preparation

Workspace preparation is an essential phase before commencing any microblading or eyebrow dermopigmentation procedure. Using the right tools to ensure a clean, safe, and hygienic environment is crucial for the client's health and well-being, as well as for the overall success of the procedure. In this paragraph, we will examine various auxiliary tools used during workspace preparation and explain their role in ensuring a safe and comfortable procedure.

One of the primary auxiliary tools used is skin disinfectant. Before starting the procedure, it is important to thoroughly clean and disinfect the eyebrow area to remove any makeup residue, oil, or dirt that could compromise the procedure's results or increase the risk of infection. Skin disinfectant is formulated to eliminate bacteria, viruses, and other pathogens, ensuring a sterile and safe environment for the procedure.

In addition to skin disinfectant, it is advisable to use sterile gauze to clean the workspace and remove any excess residue or fluids. Sterile gauze is designed to be safe and hygienic, minimizing the risk of contamination during the procedure. Ensure to use disposable gauze and change it regularly to maintain a clean and safe workspace.

Another important auxiliary tool is face protection, such as surgical masks or transparent visors. Face shields help reduce the spread of germs and pathogens in the air during the procedure and protect both the esthetician and the client from potential contaminants. It is important to wear face protection correctly and replace it regularly to maintain a hygienic and safe workspace.

Finally, using disposable gloves during the procedure is advisable to protect the hands from exposure to the client's bodily fluids and minimize the risk of cross-contamination. Disposable gloves are available in various sizes and materials and should be worn throughout the procedure, including during workspace preparation and pigment application.

Ensuring proper and appropriate use of all auxiliary tools is essential to guarantee the safety and well-being of the client during the microblading or eyebrow dermopigmentation procedure.

6. Materials for Hygiene and Safety during Procedures

During microblading and eyebrow dermopigmentation procedures, ensuring hygiene and safety is of paramount importance to protect the client's health and prevent the risk of infections or complications. In this paragraph, we will examine the specific materials used to ensure a hygienic and safe working environment, as well as best practices for handling materials during procedures.

One of the fundamental materials for hygiene during procedures is the sterile drape, or sterile field. The sterile drape is placed over the workspace to create a barrier between the client's skin and the tools and materials used during the procedure. This helps minimize the risk of cross-contamination and protects the workspace from external contaminants.

In addition to the sterile drape, it is important to use disinfectant wipes or alcohol to clean tools and work surfaces between clients. Disinfectant wipes are formulated to eliminate bacteria, viruses, and other pathogens and are particularly useful for disinfecting non-sterilizable tools such as microblading pens. It is important to follow manufacturer's instructions to ensure effective disinfection.

To ensure safety during procedures, it is important to use disposable needles and blades. Disposable needles and blades are designed to be used once and then discarded, minimizing the risk of cross-contamination and ensuring hygienic and safe results for each client. Make sure to use high-quality disposable needles and blades that comply with safety standards.

Finally, proper disposal of biological waste is important. During microblading and eyebrow dermopigmentation procedures, biological waste such as disposable needles and cleaning tissues are produced. Ensure proper disposal of biological waste according to local regulations and guidelines for managing medical waste.

Ensuring hygiene and safety during microblading and eyebrow dermopigmentation procedures is essential to protect the health and well-being of the client and maintain the highest professional standards.

7. Accessories for Client Consultation and Facial Analysis

During the client consultation and facial analysis phase, it is essential to use a range of accessories that facilitate communication and enable accurate assessment of the client's facial features. These accessories are designed to help the esthetician understand the client's preferences, evaluate the shape of the face and eyebrows, and plan the procedure appropriately.

One of the most useful accessories during client consultation is the handheld mirror. The handheld mirror allows the client to closely observe their eyebrows and communicate their preferences and expectations to the esthetician. It is important that the mirror is of good quality with a clear reflective surface to enable the client to view details accurately.

In addition to the handheld mirror, it is helpful to use measuring tools to assess symmetry and proportions of the client's face. Measuring tools may include rulers, compasses, and digital measuring devices that allow the esthetician to evaluate distances between eyebrows, eyebrow length, and other key measurements to determine the ideal shape and proportions of the eyebrows.

For a more thorough assessment of facial features, estheticians may also use latex or nitrile gloves during facial analysis. Gloves protect the esthetician's hands and allow tactile evaluation of facial features such as skin texture and eyebrow shape. Ensure to use disposable gloves and change them between clients to maintain a hygienic working environment.

Finally, it is useful to have pigment and color samples available to allow the client to view available options and choose the desired eyebrow color and shade. Pigment samples can be presented on a palette or paper strips to enable the client to compare different options and make an informed decision.

Using appropriate accessories during client consultation and facial analysis is crucial to ensure effective communication and accurate procedure planning, thereby ensuring maximum client satisfaction.

8. Specialized Tools for Corrections and Touch-Ups During the Process

During the eyebrow microblading and dermopigmentation process, various situations may arise that require corrections or touch-ups to achieve desired results. To effectively and professionally address these challenges, it is essential to have a range of specialized tools designed to correct minor errors, improve symmetry, and adjust color.

One of the most commonly used tools for corrections during the process is the angled brush. This tool features thin and compact bristles arranged at an angle, allowing the esthetician to precisely apply pigment or corrective solution to areas where adjustments to eyebrow shape or definition are needed. The angled brush is particularly useful for creating defined lines and thin hair strokes during microblading.

In addition to the angled brush, estheticians may also use correction or touch-up pens. These pens are equipped with a fine and precise tip that enables the esthetician to apply pigment or corrective solution accurately to areas requiring adjustments. Correction pens can be used to create subtle details, add definition, or modify eyebrow shape quickly and precisely.

For color touch-ups during the process, it is beneficial to use a variety of pigments and colors suitable for the client's skin tone and preferences. Pigments should be carefully selected based on skin tone, natural eyebrow color, and client's aesthetic preferences to ensure natural and harmonious results. Ensure a range of high-quality pigments and formulations suitable for various color needs are available.

Lastly, it is important to have tools available for removing excess pigment or cleaning eyebrows during the process. These tools may include cotton swabs, cotton pads, and gentle cleansing solutions that allow the esthetician to accurately remove excess pigment or residue during the procedure without compromising the final results.

Using specialized tools for corrections and touch-ups during the process is crucial to ensuring precise, natural, and satisfactory results for the client.

V. Workspace Preparation and Hygiene Measures

1. Surface Cleaning and Disinfection Procedure

Cleaning and disinfecting surfaces in the work area are essential steps to ensure a safe and hygienic environment during eyebrow microblading and dermopigmentation procedures. This process not only minimizes the risk of cross-infections but also reassures the client of your commitment to their health and well-being during the treatment.

To start, make sure you have an effective surface cleaner at hand. Choose a cleaner specifically formulated to remove pigment residues, oil, and bacteria from surfaces, ensuring a thorough and deep clean. Before beginning any procedure, thoroughly wash your hands with soap and water, using proper technique for at least 20 seconds.

Once your hands are washed, begin the surface cleaning procedure by applying the cleaner to the work area surfaces, including tables, chairs, instrument stands, and any other areas that will come into contact with you or the client during the procedure. Use a clean cloth or sponge to scrub the cleaner onto the surfaces, ensuring all areas are covered evenly.

After scrubbing the cleaner onto the surfaces, allow the product to sit for the time recommended by the manufacturer, usually a few minutes, to effectively act against bacteria and viruses. During this time, avoid touching the treated surfaces to prevent contamination.

Once the cleaner has had time to work, thoroughly rinse the surfaces with clean water to remove any cleaner residue. Use clean towels or a dry cloth to completely dry the surfaces and remove any remaining moisture.

Following the cleaning, proceed to the disinfection phase using an approved disinfectant. Ensure you carefully follow the manufacturer's instructions for diluting and properly applying the disinfectant to the surfaces. Allow the disinfectant to air dry on the surfaces for the time specified by the manufacturer to ensure effective disinfection.

After disinfection is complete, visually check that all surfaces are clean, dry, and free of any cleaner or disinfectant residues. Maintain a regular routine of cleaning and disinfecting surfaces before and after each client to ensure a safe and hygienic work environment.

2. Using Sterile Equipment During Preparation

When preparing for a microblading or eyebrow dermopigmentation session, it is crucial to ensure that all equipment used is completely sterile to guarantee client safety and prevent any risk of contamination or infection.

First, make sure you have an autoclave or another approved sterilization device to sterilize all reusable tools and equipment. The autoclave is an essential tool in any aesthetic studio, as it uses high-pressure steam and temperature to destroy bacteria, viruses, and other pathogens present on the tools.

Before starting the autoclave sterilization cycle, ensure that all tools are thoroughly cleaned with water and soap or a specific cleaner to remove any residue of pigment, oil, or other contaminants. Once cleaned, wrap the tools in sterile packaging or place them in sterilization pouches and position them in the autoclave according to the manufacturer's instructions.

During the sterilization cycle, verify that the autoclave reaches the correct temperature and pressure for the specified time to ensure effective sterilization of the tools. Once the cycle is complete, remove the tools from the autoclave using sterile gloves and handle them carefully to avoid contamination.

Before using the sterilized tools on the client, visually inspect them for any damage, such as chips or deformities, that could compromise their effectiveness or the safety of the treatment. If any tools are damaged, immediately replace them with new, sterilized ones to ensure a safe and high-quality treatment.

During the procedure, keep sterilized tools on a clean and sterile surface, avoiding contact with non-sterilized surfaces or contaminants. Use sterile gloves throughout the procedure and change them regularly to prevent cross-contamination between sterilized and non-sterilized tools.

Finally, after completing the procedure, repeat the cleaning and sterilization cycle for the tools used to prepare them for the next treatment session. Maintaining a strict sterilization protocol is essential to ensure client safety and health and to uphold the highest hygiene standards in your aesthetic studio.

3. Organization and Arrangement of Tools on the Workstation

The organization and arrangement of tools on the workstation are crucial for ensuring an efficient and safe workflow during microblading and eyebrow dermopigmentation procedures. A well-organized workstation not only facilitates your work as an aesthetician but also reassures the client of your professionalism and attention to detail.

First, ensure that your workstation is clean and orderly, free from clutter or confusion. Use appropriate containers or trays to organize tools and materials so that they are easily accessible and visible during the procedure. This setup helps avoid delays and interruptions during the treatment, allowing you to focus entirely on the client and the final result.

Arrange the tools based on their frequency of use and importance, positioning the most frequently used and essential items closest to you on the workstation. For example, microblading blades, pigments, and disinfectants should be placed prominently and within easy reach, while less frequently used items can be positioned farther away to avoid clutter.

Keep the tools well-organized and tidy throughout the procedure by repositioning them immediately after use and avoiding leaving items scattered on the workstation. This practice not only enhances your efficiency but also reduces the risk of cross-contamination and accidents during the treatment.

Use holders or tool racks to keep the tools upright and stable during the procedure, minimizing the risk of drops or spills that could damage the tools or contaminate the work area. Additionally, ensure that you regularly clean and disinfect the tool holders to maintain a hygienic and safe working environment.

Finally, at the end of each workday, take time to clean and reorganize the workstation so that it is ready for the next treatment session. Maintaining a tidy and well-organized workstation not only improves your work efficiency but also enhances the overall client experience in your aesthetic studio.

4. Hygiene Standards for the Aesthetician's Personal Cleanliness

Personal hygiene for the aesthetician is crucial for ensuring the safety and health of the client during microblading and eyebrow dermopigmentation procedures. Maintaining high personal hygiene standards not only minimizes the risk of cross-contamination and infections but also fosters a professional and welcoming work environment.

Before starting any procedure, it is essential for the aesthetician to thoroughly wash their hands with warm water and antibacterial soap for at least 20 seconds. This crucial step removes dirt, bacteria, and oils from the skin, reducing the risk of transferring germs during direct contact with the client and the tools used in the procedure.

Additionally, it is advisable for the aesthetician to wear clean, professional attire suitable for the work environment, such as aprons or long-sleeved lab coats. This protects the uniform from pigments and other contaminants and ensures a professional appearance.

During the procedure, avoid touching your face or hair with unsterilized hands, and keep hair tied back and away from the face to prevent contact with the client's skin or the tools used during the treatment.

It is also important that the aesthetician refrains from eating, drinking, or smoking during procedures and keeps nails short and clean to reduce the risk of cross-contamination. The use of jewelry such as rings, bracelets, or watches should be limited or avoided during procedures to prevent contamination of tools or the client's skin.

Finally, after completing each procedure, ensure to clean and disinfect your hands using an alcohol-based hand sanitizer or by washing them again with warm water and soap. This final step helps remove any residual pigment or contaminants from the hands, reducing the risk of transferring germs to subsequent clients.

Maintaining high personal hygiene standards is essential for ensuring client safety and satisfaction during microblading and eyebrow dermopigmentation procedures and for upholding the professional reputation of your aesthetic studio.

5. Using Workstation Protections

Workstation protections are essential for ensuring a safe and hygienic environment during microblading and eyebrow dermopigmentation procedures. These protections not only help prevent cross-contamination and the spread of pathogens but also shield the work area from pigment splashes and other contaminants.

One of the most common protections is the use of disposable covers or protective surfaces, such as paper towels, disposable sheets, or protective films, to cover and safeguard the workstation and surrounding surfaces. These covers can be easily replaced between clients, reducing the risk of cross-contamination between procedures and contributing to a clean and hygienic work environment.

Additionally, it is advisable to use protections for the tools and equipment used during procedures, such as covers for microblades, pigments, and tool containers. These protections help prevent the contamination of tools by pathogens or environmental contaminants and keep them in optimal condition to ensure high-quality results.

Workstation protections may also include the use of screens or protective barriers to separate the client from the aesthetician during the procedure, reducing the risk of direct contact and protecting both parties from potential splashes or contaminants.

Finally, make sure to use personal protective equipment such as disposable gloves and masks during procedures to protect yourself and the client from potential contamination and to maintain hygiene and sanitary standards.

In summary, using workstation protections is essential for ensuring a safe, hygienic, and professional environment during microblading and eyebrow dermopigmentation procedures, contributing to the health and safety of both the aesthetician and the client.

6. Biological Waste Disposal Procedures

Proper disposal of biological waste is crucial for ensuring safety and hygiene during microblading and eyebrow dermopigmentation procedures. Biological waste, which includes used swabs, cotton pads, tissues, and other disposable materials contaminated with blood or bodily fluids, must be managed safely and in accordance with health and environmental regulations.

Before disposing of biological waste, it is important to separate it from other waste generated during the procedure and collect it in designated containers marked as "biological waste." These containers should be durable, leak-proof, and equipped with secure lids to prevent liquid spills or accidental contamination.

Once the biological waste containers are full or at the end of the workday, they should be sealed properly and stored securely in designated temporary storage areas. These areas must be well-ventilated, clean, and separate from areas used for other purposes, such as food preparation or personal care.

Subsequently, biological waste must be removed and disposed of according to local and national regulations regarding biological waste disposal. This often involves engaging specialized medical waste collection and disposal services that are equipped to handle contaminated materials safely and appropriately.

During the transport and disposal of biological waste, it is essential to adopt appropriate safety measures, such as wearing disposable gloves and personal protective equipment, to minimize the risk of contamination and protect the health and safety of the aesthetician and those handling the waste.

Finally, it is important to keep a detailed record of biological waste disposal activities, including the types and quantities of waste generated, as well as the details of the collection and disposal services used. This record can be useful for monitoring and evaluating compliance with regulations and for identifying areas for improvement in the biological waste management process.

By following these biological waste disposal procedures accurately and diligently, you can ensure a safe, hygienic, and compliant working environment during microblading and eyebrow dermopigmentation procedures.

VI. Client Consultation and Facial Analysis

1. Introduction to the Consultation: Welcoming the Client and Setting Expectations

The initial phase of the client consultation is crucial for building trust and fully understanding their needs and expectations regarding the microblading and eyebrow dermopigmentation treatment. Welcoming the client with a warm smile and an inviting attitude is the first step in putting them at ease and encouraging open and transparent communication. It's essential to create a comfortable and relaxed environment where the client feels free to express their desires and concerns about the procedure.

During this introductory phase, the aesthetician should take the time to listen carefully to the client and ask targeted questions to understand their aesthetic expectations, goals, and personal preferences regarding the shape, color, and style of the desired eyebrows. This open and collaborative dialogue is crucial for establishing a solid foundation for the success of the treatment and ensuring the client's maximum satisfaction.

Additionally, it is important to provide the client with detailed information about the microblading and eyebrow dermopigmentation process, including potential risks and precautions to take before, during, and after the treatment. This helps to create a realistic understanding of what to expect and addresses any doubts or concerns the client may have.

Finally, it is important to clearly establish expectations regarding the anticipated results, including healing times, possible touch-ups, and long-term maintenance of the eyebrows. This allows the client to fully understand the commitment required and feel completely involved in the decision-making process.

In summary, the introduction to the consultation is a crucial moment for establishing effective communication with the client, defining their expectations, and ensuring a smooth and harmonious collaboration throughout the microblading and eyebrow dermopigmentation process.

2. Facial Morphological Analysis: Identifying Eyebrow Shape and Proportions

Facial morphological analysis is a crucial phase in the pre-treatment consultation for microblading and eyebrow dermopigmentation. This detailed process allows the aesthetician to carefully assess the client's face shape, as well as the proportions and characteristics of their existing eyebrows.

To identify the face shape, it is essential to closely observe the lines of the face, including the forehead, cheeks, chin, and jawline. This helps determine whether the client's face is oval, round, square, heart-shaped, diamond-shaped, or a combination of these shapes. Each face shape has unique features that influence the choice of the ideal eyebrow shape and style.

Next, attention is focused on the client's existing eyebrows. The aesthetician examines their shape, thickness, length, and natural arches, assessing whether they suit the client's facial morphology or if corrections or adjustments are needed.

During this phase, it is also important to consider the proportions of the face, such as the width of the nose, the distance between the eyes, and the position of the eyebrows in relation to the eyes and other facial features. This helps determine the best position and length for the eyebrows to create a harmonious and balanced appearance.

Moreover, it is crucial to actively involve the client in the facial morphological analysis, encouraging them to express their preferences and concerns regarding the desired eyebrow shape and style. This ensures a final result that meets the client's expectations and aligns with their anatomical uniqueness and personal preferences.

In conclusion, facial morphological analysis is an essential step in customizing the microblading and eyebrow dermopigmentation treatment, enabling the aesthetician to identify the optimal shape and proportions to create a natural and harmonious look.

3. Assessing Client Desires: Active Listening and Effective Communication

Assessing client desires is a crucial step in the pre-treatment consultation for microblading and eyebrow dermopigmentation. Effective communication and active listening are essential to fully understand the client's expectations and desires, as well as to establish a strong foundation for a positive and satisfactory collaboration.

During the consultation phase, it is vital for the aesthetician to dedicate time and attention to carefully listening to the client's requests and preferences. This involves not only hearing the words spoken but also understanding their emotional and aesthetic needs. Through active listening, the aesthetician can gather valuable insights into the client's style preferences, aesthetic goals, and specific concerns about the treatment.

Additionally, it is important to ask targeted questions to deepen the understanding of the client's expectations. This may include inquiries about their previous experiences with similar treatments, preferences regarding eyebrow shape, color, and style, as well as any concerns or skin conditions that might affect the treatment.

When communicating with the client, it is crucial to use clear and understandable language, avoiding technical terms that might be confusing or intimidating. Providing accurate and transparent information about expected results, potential risks, and available options allows the client to make informed decisions about the treatment.

Finally, establishing a relationship of trust and mutual respect with the client is essential, creating a comfortable and welcoming environment where they feel free to express their opinions and concerns. This contributes to effective collaboration and greater client satisfaction with the final outcome of the treatment.

In summary, assessing client desires requires a thoughtful, empathetic, and communicative approach aimed at fully understanding their needs and establishing a solid foundation for a positive and satisfying collaboration during eyebrow treatment.

4. Colorimetry Considerations: Choosing the Pigment Color Based on Skin Tone and Hair Color

Selecting the right pigment color for microblading and eyebrow dermopigmentation is crucial for achieving a natural and harmonious result. Colorimetry plays a fundamental role in determining the most suitable color based on the client's skin tone, hair color, and preferences.

First, it is important to consider the client's skin tone. People can have warm, cool, or neutral undertones, and the choice of pigment color should take this into account. Warm skin tones typically have golden or yellow undertones, while cool skin tones have pink or blue undertones. Neutral skin tones have a combination of both. Choosing a color that complements the client's skin tone will help achieve a natural result that enhances their overall appearance.

In addition to skin tone, it is important to consider the client's hair color. The shade, intensity, and hue of the hair can influence the choice of pigment color. For clients with dark hair, a slightly darker pigment might be preferable to create a more defined and pronounced eyebrow effect. Conversely, for clients with lighter hair, a slightly lighter pigment may be more suitable for a softer, more natural look.

Beyond skin tone and hair color, it is also important to consider the client's personal preferences. Some clients may want more defined and darker eyebrows, while others might prefer a softer, more blended look. It is essential to work with the client to understand their preferences and create a customized result that meets their aesthetic expectations.

In summary, selecting the pigment color for microblading and eyebrow dermopigmentation requires careful consideration of the client's skin tone, hair color, and personal preferences. A thoughtful color choice will contribute to achieving a harmonious, natural, and satisfying result for the client.

5. Defining the Work Plan: Determining the Shape and Style of the Eyebrows

Defining the work plan is a crucial phase during the client consultation. During this stage, the aesthetician must take the time to understand the client's preferences, assess the morphology of their face, and determine the most suitable shape and style for the eyebrows.

To determine the eyebrow shape, it is important to consider the client's facial structure and individual features. Eyebrow shapes can vary, including arched, straight, angular, rounded, and almond-shaped. Each shape has a different impact on the overall appearance of the face and can influence the expression and harmony of facial proportions. During the consultation, the aesthetician should carefully analyze the facial bone structure, the distance between the eyes, the nose, and the forehead dimensions to determine the eyebrow shape that best complements the client's face.

In addition to the shape, the style of the eyebrows is another key element to consider. Eyebrow styles can range from natural and soft to defined and bold, depending on the client's aesthetic preferences and desired outcome. Some clients may prefer a more minimalist and subtle look, while others may want eyebrows that are more defined and striking. During the consultation, the aesthetician should work with the client to understand their personal style and create a work plan that reflects their individual preferences.

Once the shape and style of the eyebrows have been determined, it is important to outline a clear and precise guide before beginning the treatment. This can be done using tools such as eyebrow pencils or rulers to ensure that the eyebrows are drawn symmetrically and follow the desired shape. Defining a detailed work plan will help the aesthetician achieve accurate and satisfying results that reflect the client's aesthetic preferences.

VII. Colorimetry and Color Selection

1. Principles of Colorimetry Applied to Microblading and Dermopigmentation

Colorimetry is a fundamental discipline in the field of microblading and eyebrow dermopigmentation. It is based on the scientific principles that govern the human eye's perception of colors and the theory of colors, which includes concepts such as hue, saturation, and brightness. Correctly applying the principles of colorimetry is essential for achieving optimal aesthetic results and meeting client expectations.

In the context of microblading and eyebrow dermopigmentation, colorimetry involves the accurate selection of pigments and shades to create a natural and harmonious appearance. This process requires a deep understanding of the client's individual characteristics, such as skin, hair, and eye color, as well as their personal preferences and lifestyle.

A crucial aspect of colorimetry is the ability to evaluate and compare the client's skin tones with the wide range of available pigments. This requires a trained eye and a thorough knowledge of pigment properties, including their blending capabilities and adaptability to different skin types. For example, if the client has a warm complexion, it may be necessary to use pigments with warmer tones to avoid an unnatural or ashy appearance.

Additionally, it is important to consider the natural color of the client's eyebrows and any previous microblading or dermopigmentation treatments. The choice of color should aim to enhance and harmonize the existing eyebrow shape and tone rather than overshadowing or making them unnaturally prominent.

Ultimately, applying colorimetry principles requires not only technical skills but also artistic sensitivity and an understanding of the client's aesthetic preferences. A careful and personalized approach to color selection can make the difference between a satisfactory result and an exceptional one.

2. Assessing Skin Tone and Undertones for Color Selection

Accurate assessment of skin tone and undertones is a crucial step in color selection during the microblading and eyebrow dermopigmentation process. A person's skin tone can vary widely based on factors such as ethnicity, sun exposure, and individual skin conditions. Therefore, it's essential to consider several elements when evaluating the client's complexion to ensure an aesthetically pleasing and natural result.

Firstly, it's important to observe the general skin tone, which can be classified as light, medium, or dark. This provides an initial guide for selecting the pigment color, as lighter tones may require softer pigments to avoid excessive contrast, while darker tones may need more intense pigments to achieve a visible effect.

In addition to the general skin tone, it's necessary to assess the skin's undertones, which can be warm, neutral, or cool. This can be determined by looking at the veins on the client's wrist: if they appear green, the complexion is likely warm; if they appear blue, the complexion is likely cool; if it's unclear whether they are blue or green, the complexion is likely neutral.

Once the undertones are identified, pigments can be selected that harmonize with them, enhancing the overall brightness and balance of the face. For example, people with a warm complexion may benefit from pigments with golden or brown undertones, while those with a cool complexion may opt for pigments with blue or gray undertones.

Additionally, it's important to consider any skin discolorations, such as sun spots, redness, or hyperpigmentation, which can affect color perception and pigment selection. A careful and personalized approach to assessing skin tone and undertones can significantly contribute to achieving satisfying and long-lasting aesthetic results for the client.

3. Using Color Wheels for Accurate Shade Selection

Color wheels are indispensable tools for microblading and eyebrow dermopigmentation artists, as they provide a clear and comprehensive visual representation of various shades and their nuances. These tools are designed to help artists quickly and accurately identify the shades that best match the client's skin tone and natural hair color, allowing for more precise and personalized color selection.

Color wheels are composed of a series of color samples arranged in a circular format, displaying variations in hue, brightness, and saturation around the wheel's perimeter. This arrangement makes it easy to compare different shades and tones, offering a complete overview of available options and potential combinations. Colors are generally categorized into warm, neutral, and cool groups to further simplify the selection process.

During the client consultation, using color wheels allows the artist to present various options and discuss the client's preferences in a clear and tangible way. This interactive approach fosters effective communication and helps ensure the client is involved in the decision-making process, thereby increasing overall satisfaction with the final result.

Additionally, color wheels can be used to assess the contrast between the client's skin tone and the desired eyebrow color. For example, if the client has a warm complexion, the artist might look for shades with golden or brown undertones that complement the skin. Conversely, if the client has a cool complexion, shades with bluish or grayish undertones may be preferred for a more natural and balanced appearance.

In summary, using color wheels is an essential practice for ensuring accurate and personalized color selection during microblading and eyebrow dermopigmentation. These tools provide a clear visual guide and facilitate effective communication with the client, contributing to optimal and satisfying aesthetic results.

4. Adjusting Eyebrow Color to the Client's Individual Characteristics

Adjusting the eyebrow color to fit the client's individual characteristics is crucial for achieving aesthetically pleasing and harmonious results. Each client has a unique combination of skin tone, hair color, and distinctive facial features that must be considered when selecting eyebrow color. This personalized approach ensures that the final result blends seamlessly with the client's facial features, creating a natural and balanced appearance.

During the consultation phase, it is important to carefully examine the client's individual characteristics, including their skin tone, natural hair color, and the contrast between their hair and skin. This detailed assessment provides a solid foundation for determining which eyebrow shade will best suit the client and their distinctive traits.

One key consideration is the harmony between the eyebrow color and the client's skin tone. Eyebrow shades should complement the client's complexion, avoiding excessive contrasts that may appear unnatural. For example, if the client has a warm complexion with golden undertones, it might be preferable to choose eyebrow shades with warm, golden tones for a harmonious and cohesive look.

Additionally, the client's natural hair color should be taken into account. If the client has dark hair, selecting a slightly lighter eyebrow shade can help avoid an overly heavy appearance. Conversely, if the client has light hair, darker eyebrow shades may better define and accentuate their look more effectively.

Finally, it is crucial to consider the contrast between the client's hair and skin. A moderate contrast between eyebrow color and skin tone can add definition and depth to the look, but it is important to avoid overly stark contrasts that may appear unnatural or disproportionate.

In conclusion, adjusting the eyebrow color to the client's individual characteristics requires thorough evaluation and careful selection of shades. This personalized process ensures that the final result is harmonious, natural, and aligned with the client's aesthetic preferences.

5. Advanced Techniques for Eyebrow Color Customization

Advanced techniques for eyebrow color customization represent a significant advancement in aesthetic cosmetology, allowing professionals to achieve even more precise and tailored results for individual client needs. These techniques are based on in-depth colorimetry knowledge and the use of specialized tools to create sophisticated and natural visual effects.

One of the most widely used advanced techniques is customized pigment blending. This approach allows practitioners to combine different pigment shades to achieve a color perfectly suited to the client's characteristics. By using a color wheel and a deep understanding of tonal relationships, experts can blend pigments with millimeter precision to create a unique shade that harmonizes seamlessly with the client's skin tone, hair color, and preferences.

Another advanced technique involves using translucent or semi-permanent pigments. These pigments enable practitioners to achieve a more subtle and gradual effect, ideal for clients who desire a more natural look or are unsure about the eyebrow color. These pigments can be applied in thin layers to add depth and definition without appearing too intense or stark.

The gradient shading technique is another popular option for eyebrow color customization. This technique involves applying pigment to create a gradient and gradual effect, similar to a realistic hair shading. This approach is particularly effective for clients who want a soft, natural look with a light and delicate definition of the eyebrows.

Additionally, some advanced techniques involve using corrective or neutralizing pigments to address any color irregularities in the eyebrows or to adjust undesirable hues. These pigments can be used precisely to balance unwanted undertones or correct color discrepancies, ensuring a uniform and flawless final result.

In summary, advanced techniques for eyebrow color customization offer practitioners a wide range of options to meet individual client needs. With a combination of specialized knowledge, advanced tools, and innovative techniques, professionals can create exceptional aesthetic results that enhance their clients' appearance and confidence.

6. Considerations on Duration and Color Change Over Time

Considerations regarding the duration and change of color over time are essential when selecting and applying eyebrow color. Since microblading and dermopigmentation are semi-permanent treatments, it's crucial to understand how eyebrow color may evolve over time and what factors can influence its longevity and stability.

Firstly, the quality of the pigments used and the application technique are important factors. High-quality pigments and professional application techniques can ensure greater color durability and stability over time. It is advisable to use medical-grade pigments, specifically formulated to resist fading and color changes over the months.

Additionally, informing clients about maintenance and touch-up treatments is essential. Since eyebrow color can fade over time due to natural skin regeneration and sun exposure, planning regular touch-up treatments is recommended to keep the color fresh and vibrant. These touch-ups may be scheduled every 12-18 months, depending on the client's skin type and exposure to environmental factors.

Moreover, clients should be aware that eyebrow color may experience variations over time due to factors such as sun exposure, use of skincare products, and skin aging. For instance, prolonged sun exposure can cause color fading, while the use of harsh chemical products can affect pigment stability.

It is also important to consider the client's individual preferences and current aesthetic trends. Since tastes and trends can change over time, working closely with the client to ensure the eyebrow color meets their long-term needs and expectations is crucial.

In conclusion, considerations regarding the duration and change of color over time are vital for achieving lasting and satisfactory results in microblading and dermopigmentation. Educating clients about these aspects and providing personalized advice can help ensure greater satisfaction and confidence in the final outcome.

VIII. Eyebrow Drawing and Shaping Techniques

1. Introduction to Eyebrow Drawing Techniques

The introduction to eyebrow drawing techniques marks a crucial moment in the process of defining and refining the aesthetic appearance of the face.

Eyebrows play a fundamental role in framing the eyes and defining facial expressions, significantly impacting the overall look of the face.

This chapter aims to examine in detail the various techniques used to shape and draw eyebrows to achieve aesthetically pleasing and harmonious results.

The ability to draw eyebrows appropriately requires not only technical skill but also a deep understanding of facial morphology and the client's individual preferences.

During the initial consultation, it is essential to carefully examine the client's natural eyebrow shape, considering factors such as face shape, eye placement, and overall facial proportions.

Only by fully understanding these features can one design eyebrows that harmonize with the client's features and reflect their aesthetic preferences.

In this chapter, we will explore a wide range of eyebrow drawing techniques, from pencil shaping to thread definition, providing detailed instructions, practical tips, and suggestions for achieving optimal results.

Through a combination of artistic skills and technical knowledge, microblading, dermopigmentation, and permanent makeup artists can transform the client's eyebrows into a visually appealing focal point of the face, thereby enhancing the overall appearance and boosting self-confidence.

Mastering eyebrow drawing techniques is essential for every industry professional, and this chapter aims to provide the foundational skills needed to develop these abilities successfully.

2. Morphological Assessment of the Client's Eyebrows

The morphological assessment of the client's eyebrows is a crucial step in the design and shaping process. This phase requires a thorough evaluation of the client's natural eyebrow shape, considering several key factors that influence the final result.

Firstly, it is essential to carefully examine the current shape and structure of the eyebrows, observing their length, thickness, and natural arch. These elements provide a critical foundation for determining which areas need correction or enhancement during the shaping process.

Additionally, the morphological assessment must take into account the shape of the client's face and the overall proportions. For example, a person with an oval face might need a different eyebrow shape compared to someone with a round or square face. Adapting the eyebrow design to the client's unique facial features ensures a harmonious and complementary appearance.

During the assessment, it is also important to consider the position of the eyes and the natural eyebrow arch. These elements can significantly influence how the eyebrows interact with the eyes and the overall facial structure. A well-defined eyebrow arch can help create a more youthful and lively look, while an incorrect eyebrow position might result in a tired or expressionless appearance.

In addition to the shape and structure of the eyebrows, the morphological assessment should also consider the natural color of the client's eyebrows and hair. This helps determine the best pigment shade to use during the shaping and coloring process, ensuring that the eyebrows blend naturally and harmoniously with the hair color.

In summary, the morphological assessment of the client's eyebrows is a fundamental step to ensure aesthetically pleasing and satisfying results. An accurate assessment provides the professional with the necessary information to design and shape the eyebrows in a way that enhances the client's overall appearance and meets their aesthetic preferences.

3. Identifying the Ideal Eyebrow Shape

Identifying the ideal eyebrow shape requires considering a range of factors that contribute to determining which shape will best suit the client's face and aesthetic preferences. This process involves a careful assessment of the existing eyebrow structure, as well as the proportions and shape of the client's face.

Firstly, it's important to understand that there is no universal eyebrow shape that suits everyone. The ideal eyebrow shape depends on the unique features of the client's face and their personal style. However, there are general guidelines that can help identify the eyebrow shape that will enhance the client's overall appearance.

One of the first considerations in identifying the ideal eyebrow shape is the shape of the client's face. Faces can be classified into various shapes, including oval, round, square, rectangular, and heart-shaped. Each face shape requires a specific eyebrow shape to balance proportions and enhance facial harmony.

For example, for a round face, higher-arched eyebrows can help create a more elongated and slim appearance. Conversely, for a square face, a softer, rounded eyebrow shape can help soften angular features and add definition.

In addition to face shape, it is also important to consider the position of the eyes and the client's natural eyebrow arch. These elements influence the shape and direction of the eyebrows and must be taken into account during the process of identifying the ideal shape.

During the consultation with the client, it is helpful to examine reference photos and discuss the client's personal preferences regarding eyebrow shape. This ensures a clear understanding of the client's expectations and facilitates collaboration to achieve the desired outcome.

In conclusion, identifying the ideal eyebrow shape is a process that requires a careful evaluation of the client's facial features and aesthetic preferences. Once the ideal shape is identified, the eyebrows can be sculpted to create a harmonious and complementary look that meets the client's needs.

4. Pencil Drawing Techniques: Definition and Recommended Practices

Pencil drawing techniques are a crucial aspect of eyebrow shaping, allowing permanent makeup artists to precisely define the desired shape and structure. This method offers flexibility and control during the preliminary stage of the process, enabling experimentation with different shapes and styles before moving on to more permanent techniques such as microblading or dermopigmentation.

Before starting the pencil drawing, it's important to properly prepare the workspace and ensure that all necessary tools are at hand. These tools include eyebrow pencils in various shades to match the client's natural hair color, as well as lighter pencils or markers to highlight areas that need correction or filling.

When applying the pencil technique, it is advisable to start by drawing light, thin lines along the outline of the existing eyebrows, following the natural arch of the brow. This creates a visual guide for defining the new shape and ensures a consistent and harmonious appearance.

Throughout the drawing process, it is essential to consider the client's facial proportions and aesthetic preferences. This means adjusting the shape and thickness of the eyebrows based on the face structure and desired symmetry. For instance, if the client wants a more natural look, opt for softer, lighter lines, whereas bolder, more defined lines can be used for a more dramatic effect.

Once the initial drawing is complete, it is recommended to carefully review the work and make any necessary corrections or adjustments before proceeding with more permanent techniques. This step is crucial to ensure that the client is satisfied with the final result and that the eyebrow shape is perfectly balanced and harmonious with their face.

Additionally, it's important to regularly consult the client during the drawing process, asking for their feedback and making adjustments based on their preferences. This helps ensure effective collaboration and achieves a final result that fully meets the client's expectations.

Finally, once the pencil drawing has been completed and approved by the client, the next phase of the process can begin, which may include microblading, dermopigmentation, or other permanent eyebrow shaping techniques.

5. Using Thread for Eyebrow Shaping: Procedures and Tips

Threading is an ancient technique for eyebrow shaping that remains popular due to its precision and ability to create clean, defined lines. This method requires skill and practice, but it can produce remarkable results when performed correctly.

To start, it's important to properly prepare the thread before use. A strong, high-quality cotton thread is recommended, preferably unwaxed, to ensure a secure grip and greater accuracy during the procedure. The thread should be cut to a length that is manageable and wrapped around the index and thumb fingers of both hands.

Once the thread is prepared, you can proceed with eyebrow shaping. Begin by stretching the thread between the fingers to form a narrow U-shape. Then, with quick and precise finger movements, pass the thread over the eyebrows, catching and removing unwanted hairs along the way.

During threading, it's crucial to maintain a consistent and even tension to ensure effective hair removal without causing pulling or skin irritation. It's advisable to practice on a small area before moving on to shaping the entire eyebrow, to build confidence and mastery of the technique.

Throughout the procedure, pay close attention to symmetry and the shape of the eyebrows, making sure to follow the natural arch of the brow and adjust the shape according to the client's preferences. This may require careful observation and skillful manipulation of the thread to achieve precise and harmonious results.

Once eyebrow shaping with thread is complete, evaluate the outcome and make any necessary corrections or touch-ups. Regularly consult with the client during the process, seeking their feedback and ensuring they are satisfied with the final result.

Finally, it's advisable to provide the client with detailed post-treatment care instructions, including the application of soothing creams and precautions against irritation or infection. This helps ensure an overall positive experience and maintains the eyebrows in optimal condition after shaping.

6. Hair Removal Techniques: Waxing, Tweezing, and Alternative Methods

Hair removal techniques are crucial in eyebrow shaping, offering a wide range of options to suit individual client preferences and specific needs. Among the most common methods, waxing and tweezing are widely used and provide lasting and precise results.

Waxing is a popular technique that allows for the rapid and effective removal of excess hair from the eyebrows. Before applying wax, it's important to prepare the skin with a pre-wax lotion to reduce irritation and ensure even hair removal. The wax is then heated and applied to the treatment area using an applicator, followed by a strip of fabric that is pressed onto the wax and then swiftly pulled away, removing the unwanted hairs.

Tweezing is another option for eyebrow hair removal, offering greater precision and control in removing individual hairs. Tweezers can be used to pluck hairs one by one, allowing for precise shaping and definition of the eyebrows according to the client's preferences. It's important to use high-quality tweezers with fine, sharp tips to ensure effective hair removal without damaging the surrounding skin.

In addition to waxing and tweezing, there are alternative methods for eyebrow hair removal, including threading and the use of electric devices such as trimmers and intense pulsed light (IPL) devices. Threading is a traditional technique involving a twisted cotton thread to capture and remove excess hairs, while trimmers and IPL devices offer modern solutions for quick and long-lasting eyebrow hair removal.

Regardless of the chosen method, it's essential to follow appropriate hygiene and safety procedures to ensure a comfortable and risk-free experience for the client. This includes thorough cleaning and disinfection of tools and work surfaces, as well as applying soothing and moisturizing products to reduce skin irritation and inflammation after hair removal.

7. Application of Eyebrow Cosmetics: Pencils, Gels, and Powders

Applying eyebrow cosmetics is a crucial step in defining and enhancing the shape and color of the eyebrows, contributing to a flawless and harmonious look. Among the most common products used for this purpose are pencils, gels, and powders, each offering unique benefits and adaptable to the client's preferences and needs.

Eyebrow pencils are a versatile and popular option for defining and filling in the eyebrows with precision. Available in a wide range of colors, eyebrow pencils can be used to create defined lines and fill in any sparse or less dense areas of the brows. It's important to choose a pencil that matches the natural color of the client's eyebrows and has a soft, creamy texture for easy application and a natural appearance.

Eyebrow gels are another popular choice for setting and defining the brows, offering a natural and long-lasting finish. Eyebrow gels come in various formulas, including clear gels to set existing brows without adding color and tinted gels to define and fill in the brows with an additional hue. Eyebrow gel can be applied using a specialized spoolie or an angled brush for greater precision and control.

Eyebrow powders are ideal for those who prefer a natural and blended look. Available in a wide range of shades, eyebrow powders can be applied with an angled brush to define and fill in the brows with a soft, gradual tone. Powders are particularly suitable for creating shading and dimension in the eyebrows, adding depth and dimension to the overall look.

Regardless of the chosen product, it's important to follow proper procedures for an even and professional application. This includes selecting the appropriate color based on the client's skin and hair tones, as well as using clean brushes and applicators to avoid contamination and infection. Additionally, it's advisable to set the eyebrow makeup with a clear wax or gel to ensure long-lasting wear and a flawless appearance throughout the day.

8. Eyebrow Tinting Techniques: Procedures and Considerations

Eyebrow tinting is a common practice for those looking to enhance the color and definition of their brows in a lasting way. This technique involves applying a specific color to the eyebrows to accentuate their natural hue or alter it according to the client's preferences. Eyebrow tinting methods can vary depending on the type of product used and the client's preferences, requiring precise and careful application to achieve satisfactory results.

Before starting the eyebrow tinting procedure, it is crucial to perform a thorough assessment of the client's individual characteristics, including their skin tone, hair color, and aesthetic preferences. This evaluation helps determine the most suitable color to use and customize the tinting technique to meet the client's specific needs.

During the eyebrow tinting procedure, it is important to follow the manufacturer's instructions for the tinting product being used. This includes proper preparation of the product, accurate mixing of the color, and even application on the surface of the eyebrows. Using clean and sterilized tools is essential to prevent contamination and infection during the procedure.

After applying the color to the eyebrows, it is necessary to adhere to the recommended processing time to allow the color to set properly. During this period, it is important to monitor the process closely to ensure that the color develops evenly and does not cause adverse reactions on the client's skin.

Once the processing time is complete, the color must be thoroughly removed from the eyebrows using lukewarm water and a cotton pad or a soft cloth. It is essential to remove all traces of color to avoid any residue on the skin or the eyebrows themselves.

Finally, it is important to provide the client with appropriate post-treatment instructions, including advice on how to care for their tinted eyebrows and how often to repeat the treatment to maintain the desired color over time.

Eyebrow tinting can be an effective solution for enhancing the appearance and definition of the eyebrows safely and durably, provided it is performed correctly and according to recommended procedures.

9. Final Touches and Eyebrow Maintenance Tips

Once the eyebrow shaping and styling procedure is complete, paying attention to the final touches is crucial for ensuring a flawless and long-lasting appearance. This process involves a series of final steps aimed at perfecting the shape, color, and definition of the eyebrows, as well as providing the client with useful advice to maintain the results over time.

The final touches may include correcting any irregularities or misalignments in the eyebrows, using tweezers to remove unwanted hairs and ensure a uniform and well-defined shape. This phase requires meticulous attention to detail and an expert eye to ensure that the eyebrows are impeccably groomed and harmonized with the rest of the face.

Additionally, during the final touches, any necessary color corrections can be made to ensure a natural and harmonious appearance. This may involve applying subtle shades or touch-ups to even out the color and correct any imperfections.

After completing the final touches, it is important to provide the client with practical advice for maintaining their eyebrows in optimal condition over time. These tips may include using specific eyebrow care products, such as gels or nourishing oils, to keep the hairs soft and shiny, while avoiding excessive makeup that could compromise the results achieved.

Furthermore, advising the client to avoid prolonged sun exposure and the use of harsh chemical products near the eyebrows is recommended, as this could affect the longevity and integrity of the color and shape. It is also important to inform the client about the recommended frequency for touch-ups and follow-up visits to keep the eyebrows in perfect condition over time.

Providing the client with this useful information can help them effectively care for their eyebrows and ensure lasting, satisfactory results.

IX. Practice of Eyebrow Tracing with Pencils and Stencils

1. Introduction to Eyebrow Mapping

The introduction to eyebrow mapping is a fundamental moment in defining the desired shape and style. When executed with precision and care, this practice allows for clearly outlining the contours of the eyebrows, creating a visual guide for subsequent applications of microblading, dermopigmentation, or cosmetics.

Eyebrow mapping represents the first step toward achieving aesthetically pleasing results, as it enables the customization of the work based on the unique features of the client's face. During this phase, it is essential to understand not only the morphology of the eyebrows but also the symmetry of the face, the positioning of the eyes, and other individual characteristics.

Moreover, eyebrow mapping provides an opportunity to communicate with the client and establish their aesthetic preferences. It is a moment for dialogue and sharing where you can listen to their requests, assess their needs, and offer professional advice to achieve the desired result.

In this chapter, we will explore in detail the various techniques and tools used in eyebrow mapping, providing practical instructions and useful tips for proper execution. With accurate guidance and a thorough understanding of the basic principles, you will be able to approach this crucial phase of eyebrow styling with confidence.

2. Using Pencils for Eyebrow Mapping

Using pencils for eyebrow mapping is one of the most common and versatile techniques in the cosmetic and makeup industry. This tool offers great flexibility in shaping and defining the eyebrows, allowing for precise and detailed mapping.

Before starting the mapping process, it is important to select a pencil that is suitable for the client's skin type and the desired outcome. Pencils come in various consistencies, from soft to firmer, and also differ in color and tone. It is advisable to use a high-quality pencil that is well-pigmented and easy to blend for optimal results.

During application, it is crucial to use a light and precise technique. Start by gently tracing the contours of the eyebrows, following the natural shape of the hairs. The pencil can be used to correct any irregularities or asymmetries, creating a more harmonious and balanced shape.

Another important factor is choosing the right pencil color. It is essential to select a shade that matches the natural color of the client's hair and eyebrows, ensuring a natural and harmonious result. During the initial consultation, it is a good idea to discuss the client's preferences and together determine the most suitable color.

Finally, once the pencil mapping is complete, you can use a brush to lightly blend the strokes and achieve a softer, more natural effect. This step helps to integrate the mapping with the natural eyebrow shape, creating a uniform and well-defined look.

Using pencils for eyebrow mapping requires practice and precision, but with experience and a proper understanding of the techniques, you can achieve impressive and satisfying results for the client.

3. Eyebrow Mapping Techniques with Pencils

Eyebrow mapping techniques with pencils are a crucial step in the eyebrow shaping and defining process. This method allows for precise and detailed contouring, outlining the desired shape with accuracy.

To achieve optimal results, it is important to use a series of techniques and strategies during the pencil mapping. First, start with a light and gentle line, following the natural shape of the client's eyebrows. This helps to establish the basic contours without overdoing it.

During mapping, use delicate and controlled movements, avoiding applying too much pressure on the pencil. This helps maintain an even stroke and prevents errors or overly harsh lines. Additionally, work slowly and patiently to ensure greater precision and a more natural shape.

A common technique during pencil mapping is to follow a series of predefined guidelines to define the shape of the eyebrows. These guidelines may include reference points such as the outer corner of the eye, the peak of the eyebrow arch, and the tail of the eyebrow. Following these guidelines helps maintain a harmonious and well-balanced shape.

It is also important to consider symmetry and balance between the two eyebrows. By using the pencil, you can correct any discrepancies and asymmetries, creating a uniform and balanced shape on both sides of the face.

Finally, once the pencil mapping is complete, evaluate the overall result and make any necessary corrections or adjustments. This final step ensures a consistent and well-defined appearance, meeting the client's preferences and achieving a flawless result.

4. Choosing Eyebrow Stencils for Mapping

Choosing the right stencils for eyebrow mapping is a crucial part of the process, as it determines the final shape and proportions of the eyebrows. Stencils are pre-designed tools that help achieve a uniform and well-defined shape, minimizing the risk of errors during the mapping.

Before selecting a specific stencil, it's important to carefully assess the client's facial morphology and personal preferences. Stencils come in various shapes and sizes, each designed to fit different facial features and eyebrow styles. Therefore, it's essential to choose a stencil that best matches the client's face shape and aesthetic goals.

When selecting stencils, it's also helpful to consider the symmetry and balance of the eyebrows. Ideally, the stencils should be chosen so that both eyebrows have a consistent and well-balanced shape, creating a harmonious and natural appearance.

Once the appropriate stencil is selected, it's important to position it accurately on the client's face, ensuring it is properly aligned and adheres to the desired proportions. This may require some practice and experimentation, but it is essential for achieving precise and satisfactory results.

During the mapping with stencils, it's advisable to use a pencil or eyeliner to clearly and precisely follow the contours of the stencil. It's important to work with precision and attention to detail, making sure to cover all desired areas and maintain a uniform shape throughout the perimeter of the eyebrows.

After completing the mapping with the stencil, gently remove it and evaluate the overall result. If necessary, make any corrections or adjustments using a pencil to fill in any gaps or irregularities, ensuring a flawless and satisfying final appearance.

5. Eyebrow Mapping Procedure with Stencils

The procedure for mapping eyebrows with stencils is a detailed process that requires attention to detail and precision. Before starting, ensure you have all the necessary tools, including the chosen stencils, an eyebrow pencil or eyeliner, and a fine-tipped brush for any corrections.

Start by preparing the client's facial skin by cleaning it thoroughly with a gentle cleanser to remove any makeup residue, oil, or sweat. Make sure the skin is completely dry before proceeding to ensure better adhesion of the stencil.

Next, select the appropriate stencil based on the desired eyebrow shape and the client's facial morphology. Place the stencil on the client's face, carefully aligning it and pressing it down well against the skin to avoid any gaps.

Once the stencil is in place, use the pencil to gently trace the outer contours of the stencil, following the desired shape and size of the eyebrows. Work with smooth, light movements to achieve precise and defined lines.

During the mapping, be careful to maintain a uniform shape along the entire perimeter of the eyebrows and to avoid abrupt movements that could disrupt symmetry. If needed, use the fine-tipped brush to blend any imperfections or correct minor errors.

After completing the mapping, gently remove the stencil to evaluate the overall result. If necessary, make any corrections or adjustments with the pencil or eyeliner to further define the shape of the eyebrows.

Finally, ensure clear communication with the client throughout the process, asking for feedback and confirming that the shape and proportions of the eyebrows meet their preferences. This will help ensure client satisfaction and optimal results.

6. Correction and Refinement of Eyebrow Mapping

A crucial phase in the eyebrow mapping process is correction and refinement, which allows you to perfect the shape and appearance of the eyebrows according to the client's preferences and desired aesthetic goals. After completing the initial mapping with the stencil, it's important to take the time to critically evaluate the result and make any necessary adjustments for an optimal appearance.

Start by carefully examining the eyebrow mapping, assessing symmetry, balance, and proportion relative to the rest of the face. Look for any discrepancies or irregularities and identify areas that require correction or adjustment.

Use a pencil or eyeliner to further define the contours of the eyebrows, adding details and refining the points of the start, arch, and end with greater precision. Pay particular attention to the shape of the arch and the tail of the eyebrows, ensuring they are uniform and well-defined.

During the correction process, it's important to work with lightness and precision, avoiding abrupt movements that could compromise the eyebrow shape. Use small strokes or blending to add or remove volume where necessary, creating a gradual transition between the eyebrows and the surrounding skin.

If you encounter difficulties in correcting certain areas or achieving the desired result, don't hesitate to consult the client for feedback and specific guidance on aesthetic preferences. Open and transparent communication is essential to ensure client satisfaction and achieve optimal results.

Once the correction phase is complete, reassess the overall result and make any final touches or adjustments needed to further refine the shape and appearance of the eyebrows. Ensure you devote sufficient time to this phase, as even small details can make a significant difference in the final outcome.

7. Practical Tips for Eyebrow Mapping with Pencils and Stencils

When mapping eyebrows with pencils and stencils, following some practical tips is essential for achieving precise and satisfying results. Here are some helpful suggestions to improve your technique and create well-defined and harmonious eyebrows:

Accurate Preparation: Before you begin mapping, ensure that the skin around the eyebrows is clean and free from makeup or oil residue. Use a gentle cleanser to clean the area and dry it thoroughly with a tissue.

Choosing Stencils: If you're using stencils for mapping, select those that best match the client's natural eyebrow shape and aesthetic preferences. Ensure the stencils are clean and disinfected before use to prevent contamination.

Correct Placement: Apply the stencil on the eyebrow area so that it is well-aligned with the client's eyes and face shape. Ensure that the stencil is symmetrically positioned on both sides of the face to avoid discrepancies in the eyebrow shape.

Using the Pencil: When drawing the eyebrows with a pencil, make sure to use a well-sharpened pencil for precise and defined strokes. Hold the pencil slightly angled and use gentle movements to outline the eyebrows following their natural shape.

Gradual and Precise Work: Work gradually and with precision during the mapping process, adding details and definitions bit by bit. Avoid applying too much product and try to keep a steady hand to prevent mistakes.

Correction During the Process: If you notice discrepancies or irregularities while mapping, don't hesitate to correct them immediately using a cotton swab dipped in makeup remover or a small eyebrow brush. Work patiently and attentively to achieve even and well-defined results.

Consulting with the Client: Engage the client actively during the mapping process by asking for their opinion and welcoming any feedback or suggestions. Open and transparent communication is crucial to ensuring client satisfaction and achieving results that reflect their aesthetic preferences.

By following these practical tips and dedicating time and attention to eyebrow mapping, you'll be able to achieve professional and satisfying results for your clients.

X. Local Anesthesia Techniques and Pain Management

1. Types of Local Anesthesia: Selection and Application

When it comes to local anesthesia in the context of microblading, dermopigmentation, and permanent eyebrow makeup procedures, it is crucial to understand the different types of anesthetics available and how to choose the most suitable one for each client.

Local anesthetics are medications used to temporarily numb a specific area of the body, thereby minimizing discomfort and pain during the procedure. The choice of local anesthesia depends on various factors, including the client's individual sensitivity, the expected duration of the procedure, the type of treatment, and personal preferences.

Common types of local anesthesia include topical anesthetic creams, anesthetic gels, injectable anesthetic solutions, and nerve blocks. Each type has its own advantages and disadvantages, as well as specific considerations for application and dosage.

For example, topical anesthetic creams are often used to numb the surface of the skin and are applied prior to the procedure, requiring sufficient absorption time to ensure full effect. Anesthetic gels can be used for greater precision in more sensitive areas, while injectable solutions offer deeper and longer-lasting numbness.

Nerve blocks, when appropriate, can be used to anesthetize a larger area, such as for more invasive or painful procedures. It is important to carefully assess each client and consider their needs and preferences before proceeding with local anesthesia application.

Additionally, it is essential to follow the guidelines and precautions for the use of each type of local anesthesia, ensuring the safety of the client and the success of the procedure. Proper knowledge and application of local anesthesia techniques are fundamental to providing a comfortable and satisfactory experience for the client during eyebrow treatments.

2. Pain Management in Microblading: Strategies and Protocols

When addressing pain management in the context of microblading, it is essential to adopt a range of strategies and protocols to ensure the client's optimal comfort throughout the procedure.

One of the initial considerations is the client's psychological preparation, as the anticipation of pain can significantly affect their experience during the treatment. Before starting, it is important to clearly communicate with the client about the expected levels of pain and how to manage it effectively.

In addition, the use of local anesthesia, as discussed in the previous section, is crucial for minimizing discomfort during microblading. Applying a local anesthetic before the procedure can help numb the treated area and significantly reduce the pain experienced by the client.

Besides local anesthesia, there are other practical strategies that can enhance the client's experience. For instance, selecting an appropriately sized needle can minimize pain during microblading. Thinner needles may be less painful compared to thicker ones and allow for greater precision in tracing individual eyebrow lines.

Moreover, the technician's technique can greatly influence the client's comfort level. A light and gentle touch can help reduce pain during the treatment. The technician should be mindful of the pressure applied during microblading and adjust it according to the client's needs.

Other factors to consider include the duration of the session and the possibility of taking breaks during the procedure to allow the client to relax and regain their composure. Additionally, providing emotional support and reassurance during the treatment can help reduce the client's anxiety and discomfort.

Finally, attention should be given to the post-treatment phase, with detailed instructions provided to the client on how to manage any discomfort or pain following the microblading. Proper post-treatment care can contribute to a speedy recovery and minimize discomfort after the procedure.

In summary, a combination of local anesthesia, appropriate technique, psychological preparation, and post-treatment care are crucial for effective pain management in microblading. This holistic approach ensures a comfortable and satisfactory experience for the client throughout the eyebrow treatment process.

3. Topical Anesthetics: Application and Waiting Times

The application of topical anesthetics is a crucial component in pain management during microblading and other aesthetic treatments. Topical anesthetics are designed to temporarily numb the skin, minimizing discomfort during the procedure. However, proper application is essential to ensure their effectiveness and safety.

First, it is important to choose a high-quality topical anesthetic, preferably one recommended by medical or dermatological professionals. Ensure that the product meets safety and quality standards and is suitable for use on facial skin.

Once you have selected the topical anesthetic, carefully follow the manufacturer's instructions for application. Typically, a thin layer of the anesthetic cream should be applied to the treatment area and gently massaged until fully absorbed. Avoid over-applying the anesthetic, as this could compromise the treatment results or cause unwanted reactions.

After applying the topical anesthetic, adhere to the waiting times specified in the manufacturer's instructions. This waiting period allows the anesthetic to penetrate effectively into the skin and achieve maximum numbing effect. Waiting times may vary depending on the type of anesthetic and individual skin sensitivity, so it's important to consult the manufacturer's specific instructions to determine the optimal exposure time.

During the waiting period, it is advisable to keep the treated area covered to prevent the anesthetic from evaporating and to ensure optimal absorption. Also, reassure the client about the process and address any questions or concerns they may have regarding the anesthetic application.

Once the waiting period is complete, you can proceed with the microblading or dermopigmentation procedure. It is important to monitor the client closely during the procedure to ensure that the anesthesia is providing the desired effect and that the client remains comfortable.

In conclusion, the application of topical anesthetics requires attention to detail and adherence to the manufacturer's instructions to ensure effective pain management during microblading and other aesthetic treatments.

4. Considerations for Anesthesia in Dermopigmentation: Risks and Benefits

When it comes to dermopigmentation, managing pain through anesthesia is crucial for ensuring a comfortable experience for the client. However, it is important to carefully consider the risks and benefits associated with using anesthetics in this specific context.

One of the main benefits of anesthesia during dermopigmentation is the reduction of discomfort for the client during the procedure. Dermopigmentation involves injecting pigments into the skin through micro-injections, which can be potentially painful, especially in sensitive areas like the face. Local anesthesia can help minimize this discomfort, allowing the client to feel more at ease during the treatment.

However, it is important to be aware of the potential risks associated with using anesthetics during dermopigmentation. Anesthetics can cause allergic reactions or skin irritations, particularly if the client has sensitive skin or a known history of allergies. Before using any type of anesthetic, a thorough client assessment is essential to identify any contraindications or specific health and skin concerns.

Additionally, consider the effect of anesthesia on the procedure's outcome. While anesthesia can reduce client pain, it may also affect the artist's tactile sensitivity, making it more difficult to gauge the pressure and depth of the micro-injections. This could impact the precision and accuracy of the final result.

Another important consideration is the duration of the anesthetic effect. Many anesthetics have limited efficacy over time and may require reapplication during the procedure to maintain adequate pain control. Planning accordingly and accounting for the time needed for potential reapplications during the dermopigmentation session is crucial.

In conclusion, using anesthesia during dermopigmentation can provide significant benefits in managing client discomfort. However, it is important to carefully weigh the associated risks and benefits and take appropriate precautions to ensure a safe and effective treatment.

5. Approaches to Pain Reduction During Treatment: Tips and Advice

In dermopigmentation and microblading practices, managing pain is essential to ensure client comfort throughout the procedure. While local anesthesia is commonly used to alleviate pain, there are additional approaches and strategies that can be employed to further minimize discomfort during the treatment. Here are some practical tips and advice for reducing pain during dermopigmentation and microblading:

Application of Anesthetic Creams: Before the procedure, applying anesthetic creams to the target area can help reduce client discomfort. These creams, containing anesthetic agents such as lidocaine or prilocaine, can be effective in diminishing skin pain. It is important to carefully follow the manufacturer's instructions and perform a patch test to check for any allergic reactions before use.

Breathing and Relaxation Techniques: Encouraging the client to practice deep breathing and relaxation techniques during the procedure can help decrease the perception of pain and promote a greater sense of calm and comfort. Deep, regular breaths can distract from the pain and foster a general feeling of well-being.

Ongoing Communication: Maintaining open and continuous communication with the client during the procedure is crucial for ensuring their comfort. Regularly asking the client if they are experiencing pain and if they need a break can help promptly identify any discomfort and allow for corrective measures, such as reapplying anesthetics or adjusting tool pressure.

Temperature Control: Keeping the studio at a comfortable temperature can help reduce client discomfort during the procedure. Ensuring that the studio is appropriately heated or cooled based on seasonal needs can create a more pleasant and relaxing environment for the client.

Visual Distraction: Providing the client with something to focus on during the procedure, such as relaxing music, podcasts, or a movie, can help divert attention from the pain and promote a sense of tranquility. Visual distractions can be particularly useful during the more intense phases of the procedure.

Managing Anxiety and Stress: Addressing the client's emotional needs and offering emotional support can help reduce anxiety and stress related to the procedure. Ensuring that the client feels heard, supported, and understood can contribute to a more positive overall experience and reduce pain perception.

Monitoring Individual Sensitivity: Each client has a different level of pain sensitivity, so it is important to tailor pain management strategies to their individual needs. Being attentive to the client's reactions and adopting a personalized approach can help ensure a comfortable and satisfactory experience for everyone.

Pre-Procedural Discussion: Before the procedure, it is important to openly discuss with the client the available pain management options and set realistic expectations regarding the level of comfort they can expect during the treatment. This helps build trust and transparency and allows the client to feel more prepared and confident during the procedure.

By implementing these tips and practical advice, you can significantly enhance the overall client experience during dermopigmentation and microblading, minimizing discomfort and ensuring satisfactory results.

XI. Application of the Microblading Technique

1. Preparation of Tools and Workspace

Before beginning the microblading procedure, it is crucial to ensure a thorough preparation of both the tools and the workspace. This essential step not only contributes to the client's safety but also to the precision and effectiveness of the treatment.

First, make sure you have all the necessary tools for performing microblading professionally and hygienically. These tools include disposable microblades, pigment, disposable gloves, sterile gauze, disinfectant needles, disinfectant wipes, and adhesive tape to secure the skin during the treatment. Verify that all tools are sterilized and ready for use, in compliance with hygiene and safety regulations.

Once you have prepared the tools, focus on preparing the workspace. Ensure that your work area is clean, organized, and well-lit. Eliminate any potential sources of contamination, such as dust, hair, or makeup residues, to maintain a sterile and safe environment for the client.

Arrange all tools and materials in an orderly and accessible manner, so you can use them easily during the procedure without interruptions. Organize your workstation to ensure you have enough space to move comfortably and work with precision.

Before starting the treatment, make sure to wear protective clothing, such as disposable gowns and masks, to minimize the risk of contamination and protect both yourself and the client.

Once the preparation of the tools and workspace is complete, you will be ready to begin the microblading procedure with confidence and assurance, ensuring optimal and satisfactory results for the client.

2. Preliminary Eyebrow Design

The preliminary eyebrow design is a crucial phase in the microblading procedure, as it determines the shape and symmetry of the eyebrows to be created. Before beginning the final outlining, it is essential to conduct a thorough assessment of the client's face and understand their aesthetic preferences.

Start by carefully observing the client's facial morphology, taking into account their bone structure, face and eye shape, as well as the proportions of their nose and mouth. This morphological analysis will help you determine which eyebrow shape best suits the client's facial features and what adjustments are needed to achieve a harmonious result.

Next, communicate with the client to understand their aesthetic preferences and desired outcome. Ask if they have a preferred eyebrow shape or specific requests regarding the style and intensity of the microblading. Active listening and effective communication with the client are key to ensuring their satisfaction and achieving eyebrows that perfectly match their face and style.

Once you have gathered the necessary information, proceed with the preliminary eyebrow design using a neutral-colored eyebrow pencil. Follow the guidelines established during the morphological analysis and the client's preferences to create a precise and accurate design. Employ measurement and marking techniques to ensure symmetry and balance between the two eyebrows.

During the preliminary design, also consider the natural growth pattern of the eyebrow hairs and respect their direction and inclination. This will help achieve a natural and realistic appearance once the microblading procedure is complete.

After completing the preliminary design, carefully check the shape and symmetry of the eyebrows and seek confirmation and feedback from the client. Make any necessary corrections or adjustments based on their input before proceeding with the actual treatment.

3. Choosing the Color and Shape of Microblading Blades

Selecting the color and shape of the microblading blades is a crucial step in achieving satisfying and natural-looking results. First, consider the client's natural eyebrow color and skin tone. Carefully observe the shade of their existing hair and eyebrows, as well as their facial complexion, to determine the most suitable color for the microblading blades.

Microblading blades come in various shapes and sizes, each designed to create lines and strokes of different lengths and thicknesses. The choice of blade shape and size depends on the client's aesthetic preferences, the structure of their eyebrows, and the desired outcome. For instance, thinner blades can be used to create more defined and detailed strokes, while thicker blades are ideal for filling in larger areas of the eyebrows.

Before selecting the blades, consult with the client and discuss the available options. Show them the different shapes and sizes of the blades and explain how each will affect the final appearance of their eyebrows. Ask the client whether they prefer a more natural or a more defined look and adjust your blade choice accordingly.

Also, consider the type of microblading technique you plan to use. For example, if you are opting for a hair-stroke technique, you might choose finer and sharper blades to create precise and realistic strokes. Conversely, if you are working with a shading technique, wider and flatter blades may be preferable for evenly filling in the eyebrows and achieving a gradient effect.

Finally, always check the quality and sharpness of the microblading blades before use. Ensure they are sterile and meet safety and hygiene standards to prevent infection risks or unwanted skin reactions.

4. Technique for Incision and Pigment Insertion

The technique for incision and pigment insertion is the core of the microblading process, as it determines the definition and shape of the eyebrows. Before starting, ensure you have stable control and a steady hand, as even the smallest movement can significantly impact the final result.

First, prepare the work area, making sure it is clean and well-lit. Disinfect your tools and wear disposable gloves to ensure a sterile environment. Position the client comfortably and ensure their eyebrows are completely dry and free of makeup or oil residues.

When ready to begin, select the most appropriate microblade for the type of line or stroke you wish to create. Hold the tool firmly and angle it slightly downward, maintaining a consistent angle relative to the skin. Start from the desired area of the eyebrows and gently outline the desired shape with precise, controlled strokes.

Once the shape is outlined, proceed with the skin incision using the microblade. Apply light pressure while gently dragging the blade along the predetermined path, being careful not to penetrate too deeply into the skin. Maintain a steady and fluid motion to avoid uneven lines or overly deep incisions.

After incising the skin, it's time to insert the pigment. Use a fine brush or applicator to deposit the pigment into the freshly created cuts, filling the lines evenly with small circular motions. Ensure the pigment is distributed uniformly to avoid spots or irregular areas.

Continue the process of incision and pigment insertion along the shape of the eyebrows, working with patience and precision to achieve a consistent and natural result. Periodically check your work to ensure symmetry and balance between the eyebrows.

5. Depth Control of Incisions

Controlling the depth of incisions is crucial for ensuring a safe and high-quality result in microblading. Inadequate depth can lead to pigments that are not visible, while excessive depth may cause permanent scarring and undesirable outcomes. Here are some practical tips for managing this critical aspect of the process.

First, understand that the depth of incisions depends on several factors, including the client's skin type, the thickness of their natural eyebrows, and the microblading technique used. For instance, thicker skin may require slightly deeper incisions compared to thinner skin to ensure even and long-lasting pigmentation.

During the process, use proper lighting and a magnifying mirror to constantly assess the depth of the incisions. Carefully inspect each stroke to ensure that the pigment is deposited in the correct layer of the skin, noting any color or texture variations that might indicate incorrect depth.

Adjust the pressure and angle of the microblade based on the tactile feedback and the client's skin response. A light touch is sufficient to make superficial cuts without penetrating too deeply. Maintain a steady and smooth motion, avoiding abrupt changes in direction that could compromise depth control.

Incorporate the "surface blading" technique, which involves keeping the microblade as close to the skin surface as possible without going too deep. This technique allows for better control over incision depth and reduces the risk of skin damage and scarring.

Finally, practice consistently and experiment with different techniques and tools to refine your control over incision depth in microblading. Observe the client's skin reactions and seek their feedback to continually improve your skills and achieve optimal results.

6. Creating Realistic and Natural Lines

Creating realistic and natural lines is a crucial aspect of microblading, as it helps to achieve eyebrows that look authentic and harmonious. To achieve this goal, it's essential to follow a series of targeted practices and techniques that allow for precise and well-defined strokes.

Before you begin, carefully analyze the natural direction of the client's eyebrow hairs and note their growth patterns. This observation will help you mimic the natural hair arrangement during the drawing process, ensuring a realistic and uniform appearance.

During the microblading procedure, use a light and consistent pressure to create thin, defined lines that mimic the natural hair growth. Avoid overly bold or irregular strokes, as they can appear unnatural and be difficult to blend with existing hairs.

Carefully choose the microblade most suitable for the type of lines you want to create. Microblades with different needle configurations allow for creating thinner or thicker lines, ideal for replicating the natural variety of hairs in the eyebrows.

Maintain a smooth and precise movement while drawing, closely following the shape and direction of the eyebrows. Avoid abrupt or uncertain movements that could compromise the symmetry and natural appearance of the lines.

Throughout the process, take frequent pauses to assess the result and make any necessary corrections. Use a magnifying mirror to closely examine your work and make adjustments as needed to enhance the precision and aesthetics of the lines.

Finally, remember that consistent practice is key to refining your skills in creating realistic and natural lines. Experiment with different techniques and drawing styles to find what best suits the client's needs and preferences.

7. Managing Eyebrow Symmetry and Arch

Managing eyebrow symmetry and arch is a crucial aspect of the microblading process, as it significantly impacts the final appearance and balance of the client's face. To achieve optimal results, it's essential to follow a series of targeted steps and adopt specific techniques to ensure symmetrical and harmonious eyebrows.

First, before starting the drawing, carefully assess the client's facial structure and identify any asymmetries or misalignments in the existing eyebrows. Use precise measuring tools, such as calipers or specialized instruments, to pinpoint key areas of the eyebrows, such as the start, arch, and tail, ensuring they are aligned correctly and harmoniously.

During the drawing process, pay particular attention to the shape and angle of the lines, making sure to follow the natural eyebrow structure and respect the contours of the client's face. Use clear and precise guidelines to maintain symmetry between the two eyebrows and ensure a uniform and balanced appearance.

Incorporate visual measurement techniques during the drawing process, using tools such as transparent calipers or angle guides to evaluate the arch and slope of the eyebrows and make any necessary adjustments. Be sure to also consider the client's preferences and adjust the shape and arch of the eyebrows according to their wishes and unique facial structure.

Throughout the work, take frequent breaks to evaluate progress and examine the eyebrows from different angles. Use a magnifying mirror to closely inspect the details and make any adjustments needed to enhance symmetry and overall aesthetic.

Finally, remember that consistent practice and attention to detail are essential for improving your skills in managing eyebrow symmetry and arch. Experiment with different techniques and drawing styles to develop a steady and confident hand, ensuring increasingly precise and satisfying results for the client.

8. Post-Treatment Application and Eyebrow Care Tips

After completing the microblading treatment, it's essential to provide the client with instructions and advice for proper healing and care of their eyebrows. Post-treatment application and eyebrow care tips are crucial for ensuring optimal and long-lasting results.

First, explain the essential steps for eyebrow care in the initial post-treatment phase. This includes applying a thin layer of soothing ointment or cream provided by the professional after the treatment. This will help reduce inflammation and keep the area hydrated during the healing process.

Additionally, advise the client to avoid direct sun exposure and limit the intake of substances that could affect healing, such as alcohol, caffeine, and non-steroidal anti-inflammatory drugs, unless prescribed by a doctor.

During the healing phase, it's important to keep the eyebrow area clean and dry. Suggest that the client refrain from using makeup or cosmetics in the first few weeks after the treatment and avoid touching or scratching the treated area to prevent infections or damage to the newly applied pigment.

Provide the client with detailed instructions on how to gently wash the eyebrows with water and mild soap, avoiding scrubbing the area or using harsh products that could damage the pigment.

During the healing period, it's normal for the newly treated eyebrows to experience slight color fading and possible scabbing. Reassure the client that these are normal stages of the healing process and that the eyebrow color will gradually stabilize in the weeks following the treatment.

Finally, give the client guidance on when to schedule a follow-up appointment to assess the final results of the treatment and make any necessary touch-ups or adjustments. Remind the client to follow all post-treatment instructions carefully to ensure optimal and long-lasting results.

XII. Application of Shading Technique for Fuller Eyebrows

1. Introduction to the Shading Technique for Fuller Eyebrows

The introduction to the shading technique for fuller eyebrows marks a significant advancement in eyebrow enhancement practices.

This technique, increasingly popular in the beauty industry, offers a versatile approach to achieving eyebrows that look fuller, more defined, and natural. Unlike microblading, which primarily focuses on creating fine, hair-like strokes to shape the eyebrows, shading adds depth and volume by filling in the gaps between existing hairs, creating a softer and more blended effect.

Shading allows for a range of looks, from subtle and natural to bold and defined, depending on the client's individual preferences and lifestyle.

This chapter will delve into the techniques, tools, and steps necessary for successfully applying the shading technique, providing a comprehensive guide for beauty professionals. Through detailed instructions, practical tips, and clear illustrations, readers will learn how to effectively use this technique to create fuller and more beautiful eyebrows that meet their clients' needs and expectations.

The primary goal is to provide an exhaustive overview that enables professionals to become familiar with the technique, enhance their skills, and deliver excellent results to their clients. Understanding the importance of personalized consultation is also crucial, as it involves assessing the client's individual characteristics, lifestyle, and aesthetic preferences to determine the best approach to shading.

Additionally, considerations on color selection and pain management during the treatment are addressed to ensure a comfortable and satisfying experience for the client.

With a solid grasp of this technique and the skills required to execute it with precision and care, beauty professionals will be able to expand their repertoire and offer high-quality services that meet the ever-evolving demands of the beauty market.

2. Selection of Tools and Pigments for Eyebrow Shading

Choosing the right tools and pigments is a crucial step in preparing for eyebrow shading application.

First and foremost, it's essential to select the appropriate tools with care. Basic tools include thin, flexible brushes, which are ideal for applying pigment precisely and control. It's advisable to choose high-quality brushes that ensure even color distribution and greater accuracy during application.

In addition to brushes, consider using microblades or microneedles for shading. These tools allow for the creation of fine, delicate strokes that mimic the natural appearance of eyebrow hairs, ensuring a soft and blended result. It's crucial to select high-quality, sterilized, single-use microblades to ensure safety and hygiene during the procedure.

Regarding pigments, color selection is critical for achieving natural and harmonious results. Opt for pigments specifically formulated for eyebrow shading, which have a creamy consistency and a range of colors suitable for various skin and hair tones. Prior to pigment application, perform a patch test to assess color compatibility with the client's skin tone and ensure a perfect match.

Additionally, consider the quality and safety of the pigments used. Choose pigments that comply with safety regulations and are approved by relevant authorities to minimize the risk of allergic reactions or skin irritations. Always check the expiration date of the pigment and store it correctly to ensure its effectiveness and safety before each treatment.

In summary, selecting the right tools and pigments for eyebrow shading requires attention and care. Choosing high-quality tools and safe, reliable pigments is essential for achieving excellent and satisfying results for the client. Paying close attention to every detail during the selection process is key to a successful eyebrow shading application.

3. Shading and Ombre Techniques for Fuller Eyebrows

Shading and ombre techniques are essential for creating fuller and more defined eyebrows using the shading method. These techniques add depth, dimension, and definition to the brows, resulting in a natural and realistic effect.

To start, it's important to understand the fundamental principles of shading and ombre. Shading involves the gradual application of pigment along the eyebrows, starting with a lighter tone at the base and intensifying towards the arch and tail. This process creates a soft, gradient effect that mimics the natural color transition of eyebrow hairs.

Ombre, on the other hand, involves applying pigment more concentrated and intensely in specific areas of the brows to add depth and definition. This technique is typically used to outline the arch and highlight areas of light and shadow, creating a three-dimensional effect and a more defined appearance.

When applying shading and ombre, work with light, blended movements to avoid harsh lines or color inconsistencies. Use brushes or microblades of appropriate size to ensure precise and controlled pigment application. Additionally, varying the pressure and angle of the tool can create a range of strokes and gradations, adding interest and depth to the final result.

Another important aspect of shading and ombre techniques is pigment color selection. Choose a color that matches the natural hair and skin tone of the client, ensuring that the final result is harmonious and complements their overall look. Performing patch tests and assessing color compatibility with the client's complexion before application is crucial for achieving optimal results.

In summary, shading and ombre techniques are powerful tools for creating fuller and more defined eyebrows using the shading method. Understanding the basic principles and regularly practicing these techniques are essential for improving your skills and delivering exceptional results for clients. Paying attention to details, from color selection to application technique, is key to ensuring a natural and satisfying eyebrow appearance.

4. Step-by-Step Procedure for Applying Eyebrow Shading

Here is a detailed step-by-step procedure for applying shading to eyebrows:

1. **Prepare the Work Area:** Start by ensuring that the work area is clean, disinfected, and well-lit. Organize all necessary tools and materials, including pigments, brushes, disinfectants, and disposable supplies.

2. **Consultation with the Client:** Before beginning, consult with the client to understand their aesthetic preferences and expectations regarding their eyebrows. Assess their skin type, complexion tone, and face shape to determine the most suitable color and style.

3. **Preliminary Eyebrow Design:** Use a pencil to draw a preliminary guide for the eyebrows, considering the desired shape and natural arch. This drawing will serve as a reference during the shading application.

4. **Prepare Tools and Pigments:** Select the appropriate microblades or brushes based on the preferred shading technique and desired details. Mix the pigments to achieve the desired shade and ensure you have a range of tones to add depth and dimension.

5. **Apply the Pigment:** Start by applying the pigment along the outline of the eyebrows using light, blended strokes. Focus on areas that need more definition and fullness, such as the arch and tail of the eyebrows. Gradually blend the pigment towards the base of the eyebrows, creating a soft and natural transition effect.

6. **Build Color and Shape:** Continue adding layers of pigment, alternating between lighter and darker shades to create a three-dimensional effect and a more realistic appearance. Pay attention to the symmetry and balance of the eyebrows, adjusting the amount and distribution of pigment as needed.

7. **Check Incision Depth:** Adjust the pressure and angle of the tool to control the depth of the incisions and ensure an even application of pigment. Avoid penetrating too deeply into the skin to prevent excessive bleeding and to enhance healing.

8. **Finish and Refine:** Once shading is complete, carefully check the final result and make any necessary corrections or touch-ups. Use a sterile cotton pad to clean any excess pigment and assess the symmetry and overall appearance of the eyebrows.

9. **Post-Treatment Instructions:** Provide the client with detailed post-treatment care instructions, including recommended products, expected healing times, and precautions to maintain the eyebrows in optimal condition.

10. **Follow-Up Appointment:** Schedule a follow-up appointment with the client to assess the final result, answer any questions, and discuss any necessary touch-ups or adjustments.

By following this step-by-step procedure with attention and precision, you will be able to apply eyebrow shading effectively and professionally, ensuring satisfying results for your clients.

5. Managing Color and Shape During Eyebrow Shading Application

During the application of eyebrow shading, managing color and shape plays a crucial role in achieving optimal results and meeting client expectations. Here are some key aspects to consider for effective and harmonious application:

1. **Analyze the Natural Eyebrow Color:** Before starting the treatment, carefully assess the client's natural eyebrow color. This will help determine the pigment shade to use and ensure a final result that blends seamlessly with the rest of the face.

2. **Choose the Right Pigments:** Select a range of pigments that match the client's skin tone and hair color. Opt for pigments with good longevity and blending capabilities to create natural and realistic shades.

3. **Color Gradation:** During shading, work with various tones to create a three-dimensional effect and a gradual transition from the eyebrow outline to the base. Use darker shades to define the outline and gradually add lighter tones towards the base for a more natural look.

4. **Create Realistic Gradients:** Focus on creating subtle, realistic gradients that mimic the natural appearance of eyebrow hairs. Use a light, blended shading technique to avoid harsh lines or uneven color, ensuring a uniform and natural appearance.

5. **Respect the Eyebrow Shape:** Carefully follow the natural shape of the client's eyebrows during shading. Adhere to the natural arch and hair growth direction to achieve a harmonious and flattering look.

6. **Check Symmetry:** Use measurement tools and markers to ensure symmetry during shading. Regularly check the shape and length of the eyebrows to correct any discrepancies and ensure a balanced and harmonious final result.

7. **Adjust Based on Client Preferences:** Throughout the treatment, engage with the client to assess their aesthetic preferences and make real-time adjustments. Ask for feedback on color, shape, and shading intensity to ensure maximum client satisfaction.

8. **Finish and Touch-Ups:** After completing the shading application, perform a final touch-up to correct any imperfections or irregularities. Make any necessary adjustments to ensure a flawless and long-lasting final result.

By following these steps and paying attention to detail, you will be able to successfully manage color and shape during eyebrow shading application, achieving satisfying and high-quality results.

6. Correction and Refinement of Eyebrows After Shading Application

After applying shading to the eyebrows, it's crucial to focus on correction and refinement to ensure a flawless final result. Here are some steps to follow for correcting any imperfections and perfecting the appearance of the eyebrows:

1. **Assess Asymmetry:** Before starting the correction, carefully evaluate any asymmetry and discrepancies in the eyebrows. Use measurement tools and markers to identify correction points and establish a guideline for your work.

2. **Touch Up Uneven Pigmented Areas:** If some areas remained unevenly pigmented or showed irregularities during shading, use a targeted filling technique to correct these zones. Apply additional pigment with light pressure to achieve an even distribution and a uniform tone.

3. **Define the Contour:** Use a pencil or eyeliner to precisely define the eyebrow contour. Draw a thin line along the outer edge of the eyebrows to enhance their definition and correct any irregularities in the outline.

4. **Blend for a Natural Transition:** After defining the contour, use a spoolie or a soft-bristled brush to gently blend the pigment along the edge of the eyebrows. This will help create a gradual transition between the pigment and the surrounding skin, resulting in a more natural and harmonious look.

5. **Correct Hard Lines:** If hard or irregular lines were created during shading, use a soft brush to gently blend the pigment and soften the more pronounced lines. Work lightly and precisely to achieve a smooth and natural effect.

6. **Check Symmetry:** Once the correction is complete, carefully check the symmetry of the eyebrows using measurement tools and markers. Ensure both eyebrows are balanced and harmonious, making any necessary adjustments to correct discrepancies.

7. **Client Consultation:** Throughout the correction and refinement process, consistently involve the client to gauge their satisfaction and make adjustments based on their aesthetic preferences. Request feedback on color, shape, and shading intensity to ensure complete client satisfaction.

8. **Apply Setting Gel and Provide Care Instructions:** After completing the correction and refinement, apply a transparent setting gel to extend the pigment's longevity and protect the eyebrows from daily wear. Provide the client with post-treatment care advice, such as avoiding direct sun exposure and using gentle cleansing products, to ensure optimal and long-lasting healing.

By following these steps with care and precision, you will be able to correct and refine the eyebrows after shading application, achieving a flawless and satisfying final result for the client.

7. Post-Treatment Care Tips for Shaded Eyebrows

After undergoing the shading technique for eyebrows, it is essential to provide the client with post-treatment care instructions to ensure optimal healing and prolong the longevity of the results. Here are some practical tips to follow:

1. **Avoid Direct Sun Exposure:** In the days following the treatment, advise the client to avoid direct sun exposure and the use of tanning beds. Direct sunlight can cause premature fading of the pigment and compromise the final outcome.

2. **Avoid Contact with Water:** For the first few days after the treatment, recommend avoiding direct contact of the eyebrows with water and moisture. This includes avoiding washing the face directly over the eyebrows and refraining from swimming in pools or the sea. Water and moisture can affect the pigment's stability and slow the healing process.

3. **Avoid Skincare Products:** During the healing period, suggest that the client avoid using skincare products containing harsh ingredients, such as exfoliating acids or lightening agents. These products can irritate the skin and compromise the pigment's stability.

4. **Avoid Makeup on the Treated Area:** In the initial days after the treatment, advise against applying makeup on the treated area. Makeup can clog pores and interfere with the healing process, affecting the final result.

5. **Avoid Rubbing or Scratching the Eyebrows:** During the healing period, recommend that the client avoid rubbing or scratching the eyebrows. This can cause irritation and remove the freshly applied pigment, compromising the final result.

6. **Apply Soothing and Moisturizing Creams:** Recommend applying soothing and moisturizing creams to the treated area to relieve any discomfort and support the healing process. Ensure that the creams used are gentle and free from irritating ingredients.

7. **Follow Professional Instructions:** Finally, remind the client to carefully follow all instructions provided by the professional during the treatment session. These instructions are designed to maximize results and ensure optimal healing.

By diligently following these post-treatment care tips, the client will be able to maintain their shaded eyebrows in optimal condition and enjoy long-lasting, satisfactory results.

8. Expected Results and Possible Risks Associated with the Shading Technique

When applying the shading technique to achieve fuller eyebrows, it is crucial to understand both the expected results and the potential risks associated with the treatment.

Expected Results: The shading technique aims to create a natural and defined appearance for the eyebrows, with increased density and fullness. It effectively fills in gaps and corrects asymmetries, ensuring a uniform and harmonious result. Additionally, shaded eyebrows can enhance facial expression and highlight features, giving a more youthful and refreshed look.

Potential Risks: However, it's important to be aware of the possible risks involved with the treatment. One risk is the potential for allergic reactions to the pigment used, which may present as redness, itching, or swelling in the treated area. Performing a patch test prior to the treatment is essential to rule out any allergies.

Another risk is the possibility of infections, particularly if hygiene standards are not strictly followed during the procedure. It is crucial to use sterilized tools and adhere to recommended hygiene practices to prevent any risk of infection.

Additionally, complications may arise during the healing process, such as scab formation or partial pigment loss. These complications are typically temporary and can be managed with proper care during the post-treatment period.

Finally, it's important to recognize that the final outcome of the treatment also depends on individual characteristics, such as skin type and healing process. Some clients may achieve better results than others and might require additional touch-up sessions to reach the desired outcome.

In conclusion, while the shading technique offers significant benefits for achieving fuller and more defined eyebrows, it is essential to be aware of the potential risks associated with the treatment and take the necessary precautions to minimize them, ensuring safe and satisfying results.

XIII. Corrections and Touch-ups in Microblading and Dermopigmentation

1. Touch-Up Procedures in Microblading and Dermopigmentation

Touch-ups in microblading and dermopigmentation are a crucial phase to ensure satisfactory and long-lasting results. This procedure is performed to correct any imperfections or update the color and shape of the eyebrows over time. During a touch-up, minor adjustments are made to maintain the natural appearance of the eyebrows and align them with the client's preferences.

One of the first considerations during a touch-up is to carefully assess the previous work and identify areas that need correction or improvement. This phase requires a thorough examination of the existing eyebrows, analyzing their shape, color, and density. It is also essential to consider any changes in the client's appearance, such as variations in skin color or aesthetic preferences, to adjust the treatment accordingly.

Once the areas requiring touch-up are identified, it's important to plan the strategy carefully. This may involve choosing new pigment shades to enhance the eyebrow color or modifying the shape to achieve a more harmonious and natural look. Effective communication with the client during this phase is crucial to fully understand their needs and ensure complete satisfaction with the final results.

During the touch-up, the technician must demonstrate great skill and precision in handling tools and applying pigment. This requires a steady hand and a solid understanding of microblading and dermopigmentation techniques. Additionally, attention must be paid to the depth and angle of the incisions or pigment applications to achieve uniform and natural results.

Once the touch-up is complete, it's essential to provide the client with appropriate post-treatment care instructions. This may include guidance on how to cleanse and moisturize the eyebrows, as well as advice on what to avoid to ensure optimal healing. Furthermore, scheduling a follow-up appointment is advisable to evaluate the results and make any additional corrections if needed.

In conclusion, touch-up procedures in microblading and dermopigmentation require careful planning, technical and communicative skill, and appropriate post-treatment care. When executed correctly, these touch-up sessions help maintain fresh and natural-looking eyebrows over time, meeting the aesthetic needs of clients.

2. Identifying Areas to Correct

Accurate identification of areas to correct is a crucial step in the touch-up process for microblading and dermopigmentation. This phase requires a detailed and thorough evaluation of the existing eyebrows, along with a deep understanding of the client's aesthetic preferences.

To identify the areas that need correction, the technician must carefully examine the shape, color, and density of the eyebrow hairs. This includes looking for any discrepancies in symmetry, irregular lines or breaks in the hair strokes, and assessing the pigment distribution on the skin. It is important to note any areas that need correction or updating, considering the client's individual preferences and desired aesthetic goals.

Effective communication with the client during this phase is essential. The technician should openly discuss the client's concerns and expectations regarding the touch-up. This may involve reviewing before-and-after photos from the previous treatment and discussing any desired changes in the eyebrow appearance.

Once the areas to correct have been identified, it is important to carefully plan the treatment and establish a clear action plan. This might include selecting specific correction techniques, choosing appropriate pigments, and defining clear goals for the final result. During the planning phase, the technician should take into account the skin's limitations and the client's individual characteristics, ensuring a personalized approach to achieve the best possible results.

In conclusion, accurate identification of areas to correct is a crucial step in the touch-up process for microblading and dermopigmentation. This phase involves careful evaluation of the existing eyebrows and effective communication with the client to ensure satisfying results that align with their aesthetic preferences.

3. Color Correction Techniques

Color correction techniques are a crucial aspect of the touch-up process in microblading and dermopigmentation. These techniques are designed to address any discrepancies in the color of existing eyebrows or previous pigment applications to achieve a uniform and harmonious appearance.

One of the most common color correction techniques is adjusting the pigment tone. This may be necessary if the eyebrow color appears too light, too dark, or has undesirable undertones. To correct the tone, the technician can mix different pigments to create a custom shade that better matches the client's complexion and preferences. It's important to consider the skin's undertones and the natural hair color to achieve natural and harmonious results.

Another technique for color correction is neutralizing unwanted tones. This might be required if the previous pigment has developed reddish, grayish, or greenish hues over time. To neutralize these tones, the technician can use complementary pigments to correct the undesirable hue and restore a natural and even color.

In some cases, it may be necessary to completely remove the existing pigment before applying a new color. This can be done using pigment removal techniques such as laser treatment or saline removal. Once the unwanted pigment is removed, the technician can then apply a new color using microblading or dermopigmentation techniques.

It's essential to perform these techniques with extreme precision and care to avoid undesired results. The technician should carefully evaluate the existing eyebrow color, surrounding skin, and the client's preferences before proceeding with any color correction. Practice and experience are key to achieving optimal and satisfying results for the client.

4. Methods for Adjusting Eyebrow Shape

There are several methods available for adjusting eyebrow shape during the correction and touch-up process in microblading and dermopigmentation. Each method has its own characteristics and can be used based on the client's specific needs and desired outcome.

One of the most common methods for adjusting eyebrow shape is freehand shaping. This technique allows the technician to manually draw the desired shape of the eyebrows using a microbrush or a similar tool. This method provides maximum flexibility and precision, enabling the technician to create custom shapes that fit the client's unique facial features.

Another popular method is the use of stencils or templates to define the eyebrow shape. Stencils come in various shapes and sizes and can be used to achieve symmetrical and precise forms. The technician can place the stencil on the client's eyebrows and then apply the pigment following the stencil's outline to create a uniform and well-defined shape.

In some cases, it may be necessary to use waxing techniques to remove unwanted hairs and adjust the eyebrow shape. This method is particularly useful for correcting irregular or excessively sparse eyebrows, allowing the technician to create a more defined and even shape.

Microblading or dermopigmentation techniques can also be employed to adjust the shape of the eyebrows during the touch-up process. These techniques allow the technician to add hairs or pigment to desired areas to create a fuller and more defined shape. This method is especially useful for correcting any irregularities or asymmetries in existing eyebrows.

Regardless of the method used, it's crucial to perform the shape adjustment with precision and care to achieve optimal and satisfying results for the client. The technician should take the time to carefully assess the existing eyebrow shape and the client's preferences before proceeding with any corrections.

5. Managing Scars and Asymmetries

Managing scars and asymmetries during the correction and touch-up process in microblading and dermopigmentation requires a careful and targeted approach to ensure satisfactory and natural results.

When dealing with scars on the eyebrows, it is essential to carefully assess their size, shape, and location before proceeding with any correction. Scars can significantly affect the appearance of the eyebrows and may require a customized approach to achieve optimal results.

One technique used to manage scars on the eyebrows involves applying pigment to the scarred areas to camouflage them and make them less noticeable. This can be done using microblading or dermopigmentation techniques to add hairs or pigment to the affected areas and create a gradual transition between the scarred areas and the rest of the eyebrows.

In some cases, it may be necessary to use camouflage techniques to completely conceal the scars on the eyebrows. This can be achieved by using special pigments and blending techniques to create a uniform effect that integrates well with the natural color of the surrounding eyebrows.

When addressing asymmetries in the eyebrows, it is important to carefully evaluate the differences in shape and size between the two eyebrows and develop a personalized correction plan to achieve a harmonious and natural symmetry.

One technique used to correct asymmetries involves using measurement and marking techniques to identify discrepancies between the eyebrows and determine the best correction strategy. This may include adding hairs or pigment to under-sized areas or removing hairs or pigment from over-sized areas to achieve a more balanced and harmonious shape.

Regardless of the technique used, it is crucial to take the time to carefully assess the scars and asymmetries of the eyebrows and develop a customized treatment plan for each client. A thoughtful and targeted approach can help ensure satisfying and natural results that enhance the overall appearance of the eyebrows.

6. Tips for an Effective and Long-Lasting Touch-Up

To achieve an effective and long-lasting touch-up in microblading and dermopigmentation, it's crucial to follow some practical tips that can make a significant difference in the final appearance of the eyebrows.

First, it's important to consider the time elapsed since the last treatment and carefully assess the current state of the eyebrows before proceeding with the touch-up. This can affect the amount of residual pigment and the shape of the eyebrows, determining the type and extent of the touch-up needed.

Before starting the touch-up, it's advisable to thoroughly clean the eyebrow area to remove any makeup, oil, or sweat that might affect the pigment's adhesion. This ensures a clean and prepared surface for the treatment, optimizing the final results.

During the touch-up, it's important to use the same tools and pigments that were used during the initial treatment to ensure consistency in color and texture of the eyebrows. This helps avoid discrepancies in color or shape between the new applications and the previously treated areas, ensuring a uniform and natural appearance.

Additionally, it's advisable to closely follow the technician's instructions during the touch-up and communicate any specific concerns or desires regarding the final result. Open and transparent communication with the technician can help ensure that the client's expectations are met and any necessary corrections are made during the treatment.

After the touch-up, it's important to follow the post-treatment instructions provided by the technician to ensure proper healing and extend the longevity of the results. This may include avoiding direct sun exposure, avoiding contact with chlorinated or salty water, and applying specific moisturizing creams to keep the eyebrows hydrated and protected.

Finally, it's advisable to schedule periodic touch-ups to maintain the appearance of the eyebrows over time and ensure they are always in top shape. This can help keep a fresh and natural look and extend the duration of the results.

XIV. Managing Clients with Scars or Dermatological Conditions

1. Assessment of Scars and Dermatological Conditions

Assessing scars and dermatological conditions is a crucial step in managing clients who wish to undergo microblading, dermopigmentation, or permanent makeup treatments for their eyebrows.

Before starting any procedure, it is essential to conduct a thorough analysis of the scars present on the face or the skin conditions that may affect the final outcome of the treatment.

Scars can vary widely in size, shape, and type, from acne scars to surgical scars, and they can present unique challenges during the pigmentation process.

Similarly, dermatological conditions such as dermatitis, psoriasis, or vitiligo can influence how the skin responds to the pigment and its ability to retain color over time.

To ensure optimal results and client safety, it is crucial to carefully assess these conditions before proceeding with the treatment, taking necessary measures to mitigate any risks and adapting the technique according to the specific characteristics of the client's skin.

A comprehensive assessment also helps in setting realistic expectations for the client and providing appropriate advice on the most suitable treatment options for their individual needs.

In this chapter, we will explore in detail the strategies and considerations to keep in mind when managing clients with scars or dermatological conditions, to ensure satisfactory results and an overall positive experience.

2. Specialized Approaches for Scar Management

In the context of managing clients with scars, it is crucial to adopt specialized approaches that account for the specific characteristics of each skin lesion.

One of the initial steps is to understand the type and severity of the scar. Scars can be hypertrophic, keloid, atrophic, or linear, and may result from surgical procedures, trauma, or dermatological conditions such as acne. Each type of scar requires a unique approach, as it can affect how the skin reacts to pigment and its ability to retain color over time.

For hypertrophic or keloid scars, for example, special attention is needed in selecting the pigment and determining the depth of the incisions during treatment to avoid excessive stimulation of the scar tissue. In contrast, atrophic scars may require a more delicate approach to ensure adequate pigmentation and an even consistency of the eyebrows.

Additionally, it is important to consider the scar's location and its interaction with the natural lines of the face. Scars close to the eyebrow area may require a more precise pigmentation technique to effectively blend them, while those positioned outside the eyebrow area may influence the design choice and the arrangement of strokes.

Using specialized pigments designed for scars and consulting with a dermatologist or plastic surgeon can be helpful in identifying the best approach for each individual case. Open and transparent communication with the client is also essential, allowing for realistic expectations to be set and ensuring maximum satisfaction with the final treatment results.

In this chapter, we will explore a range of specific strategies and techniques for effectively and safely managing scars, providing practical advice and guidelines for achieving optimal results in more complex situations.

3. Considerations During the Pre-Treatment Consultation

During the pre-treatment consultation with clients who have scars or dermatological conditions, it is essential to adopt a thorough and attentive approach to carefully assess their specific needs and concerns.

First, it is important to gather detailed information about the client's medical history, including any pre-existing skin conditions, past surgeries, previous dermatological treatments, and known reactions to skin pigmentation. This information allows the professional to fully understand the client's skin status and identify any potential risk factors or complications that could affect the treatment.

Next, a comprehensive visual examination of the client's scars or dermatological conditions is crucial. This may include assessing the size, shape, texture, and color of the scars, as well as noting any irregularities or asymmetries in the skin's surface. In some cases, it may be necessary to use a magnifying glass or special lighting to closely examine the affected areas and identify any relevant details.

During the consultation, it is also important to listen attentively to the client's concerns and discuss realistic treatment expectations. This is an opportunity to establish open and transparent communication, educating the client about possible treatment outcomes and limitations associated with their specific conditions. It also allows the professional to develop a personalized plan that takes into account the client's aesthetic preferences and the unique characteristics of their skin.

Finally, it is essential to provide the client with all the necessary information to make an informed decision about the treatment. This includes discussing potential risks and benefits, available alternatives, and recommended post-treatment precautions to maximize results and minimize the risk of complications. A thorough and accurate consultation ensures that the client feels comfortable and confident in proceeding with the treatment and helps establish a strong foundation for effective collaboration between the professional and the client.

4. Specific Techniques for Scars and Dermatological Conditions

When treating scars and dermatological conditions, it is crucial to adopt specific techniques to achieve optimal results and ensure the client's safety and comfort.

One of the most commonly used techniques is applying various pigmentation methods to correct skin irregularities. For example, with hypertrophic or keloid scars, which may be raised above the surrounding skin, it is often advisable to use microblading or dermopigmentation techniques to create gradual shades that mimic the natural skin texture and help reduce the appearance of elevation.

For hypopigmented or hyperpigmented scars, which exhibit lighter or darker pigmentation compared to the surrounding skin, it is important to select appropriate pigments and use precise blending techniques to achieve an even and natural color. Additionally, shading or ombre techniques can be employed to mask color differences and enhance the overall appearance of the skin.

In cases of dermatological conditions like vitiligo or alopecia areata, which cause pigment loss or thinning of eyebrow hairs, dermopigmentation can be used to restore pigmentation or create the illusion of individual hairs. In these instances, working with extreme precision and care is essential to ensure natural and harmonious results.

Special precautions should also be taken during the treatment of scars or dermatological conditions, such as avoiding direct work on the most sensitive or irritated areas of the skin and using appropriate needles and tools to minimize the risk of additional damage or irritation.

Finally, it is advisable to customize each treatment based on the client's specific needs and individual characteristics, considering the skin type, color, and size of scars, as well as personal aesthetic preferences. A thorough consultation and accurate assessment before the treatment are essential to determine the best strategy and ensure satisfactory and long-lasting results.

5. Post-Treatment Care Tips for Clients with Scars or Dermatological Conditions

After undergoing microblading or dermopigmentation for scars or dermatological conditions, it is crucial to provide clients with comprehensive and detailed post-treatment care instructions to ensure optimal healing and lasting results.

First, it's important to inform clients about preventive measures to avoid potential complications during the healing process. This includes advising them to avoid direct sun exposure and excessive heat, as well as steering clear of harsh cosmetics or cleansers on the treated areas.

Additionally, clients should be advised to avoid direct contact with water and steam for at least 24-48 hours after the treatment to allow the skin to heal without external interference. During this time, it is also important to refrain from scratching or rubbing the treated areas, as this could compromise the final result and increase the risk of infection.

Clients should also be given detailed instructions on how to apply any recommended healing creams or ointments to accelerate the healing process and reduce the risk of inflammation or infection. These products should be applied gently to the treated skin as per the professional's guidelines.

During the healing period, clients should keep the skin moisturized and protected by using gentle, fragrance-free, and dye-free moisturizers. This can help prevent dryness and peeling, promoting faster and more even healing.

Finally, it is important to schedule a follow-up appointment with the client to assess the treatment results and provide any additional advice or corrections if necessary. During this follow-up visit, the professional can also offer further instructions for long-term care of the scars or dermatological conditions treated to maintain results over time.

Providing a thorough and personalized post-treatment care guide is essential for ensuring client satisfaction and achieving optimal long-term results.

XV. Precautions and Safety in Performing Procedures

1. Use of Personal Protective Equipment (PPE)

The chapter on "Use of Personal Protective Equipment (PPE)" delves into essential practices for ensuring safety and hygiene during microblading, dermopigmentation, and eyebrow permanent makeup procedures.

Proper use of PPE is a crucial precaution to protect both the technician and the client from potential health risks. These devices include a wide range of equipment, such as disposable gloves, face masks, protective gowns, and safety goggles.

Disposable gloves provide a critical barrier to prevent cross-contamination and the transmission of pathogens. It's important to use gloves suitable for contact with bodily fluids and to change them regularly during the procedure.

Face masks are essential for reducing exposure to particles, vapors, or aerosols that may arise from the use of chemicals or pigments. Wearing an appropriate mask protects the technician from potential irritations or damage to the respiratory system.

Protective gowns offer an additional layer of defense against contamination and stains. Choosing high-quality gowns helps maintain a clean and hygienic working environment, reducing the risk of cross-contamination.

Safety goggles are indispensable for protecting the eyes from exposure to splashes of pigments or other liquids during procedures. Ensuring eye safety is crucial to prevent injuries or irritations that could compromise the well-being of both the technician and the client.

Implementing these precautions, along with proper selection and replacement of PPE, contributes to creating a safe, hygienic, and professional working environment. Investing in personal protection not only safeguards the health of those performing the procedures but also that of the clients, ensuring a positive and risk-free experience.

2. Sterilization and Disinfection of Tools

Sterilization and disinfection of tools are fundamental pillars for ensuring safety and hygiene during microblading, dermopigmentation, and eyebrow permanent makeup procedures.

Sterilization is the process that eliminates all microorganisms present on tools, including bacteria, viruses, and fungi. This is typically achieved using autoclaves, which employ high-temperature steam under pressure to destroy pathogens. It is crucial to strictly follow the manufacturer's instructions to ensure effective sterilization of the tools.

Disinfection, on the other hand, is the process that reduces the presence of pathogenic microorganisms on tools but does not necessarily eliminate them completely. Various disinfection methods include immersion in chemical disinfectant solutions, the use of ultrasonic devices, and cold sterilization. It is essential to choose the most appropriate disinfection method based on the type of tool and regulatory guidelines.

During the sterilization and disinfection of tools, attention must be paid to several factors, such as the contact time with the disinfectant, proper dilution of solutions, and the correct operation of sterilizing equipment. Using high-quality tools that can withstand sterilization processes without damage or deterioration is also important.

Additionally, it is crucial to adopt safe handling practices for tools during procedures, avoiding direct contact with non-sterilized parts and ensuring that tools are used only on areas that have been properly treated and prepared.

Investing time and effort in the sterilization and disinfection of tools is an essential step in ensuring the safety and health of both the technician and the client. Rigorous adherence to hygiene and sterilization procedures helps create a professional and reliable environment where the quality of service is paramount.

3. Work Environment Control

Controlling the work environment is crucial for ensuring the safety and effectiveness of microblading, dermopigmentation, and eyebrow permanent makeup procedures. This involves a series of proactive measures designed to create an optimal and secure environment for both the client and the technician.

Firstly, it is essential to ensure that the work environment is clean and well-organized. This means keeping work areas, tools, and surfaces clean and regularly disinfected, minimizing the risk of cross-contamination and the spread of pathogens.

Additionally, it is important to constantly monitor and control the temperature and humidity levels in the work environment. Conditions that are too hot or humid can negatively affect the stability and performance of the pigments used during procedures, while environments that are too cold can make the client uncomfortable and compromise the technician's precision.

Another key consideration is the management of waste and contaminated materials. It is essential to have appropriate containers for the safe disposal of used needles, disposable gloves, and other contaminated materials. This helps to reduce the risk of infections and the spread of pathogens in the work environment.

Furthermore, it is advisable to maintain a detailed record of all materials used during procedures, including pigments, disinfectants, and other chemicals. Tracking this information helps monitor material usage and consumption, as well as ensures compliance with safety and hygiene regulations.

Finally, it is important to adequately educate and train staff on the importance of work environment control and the adoption of best hygiene and safety practices. This may include attending specific training courses on workplace hygiene and safety, as well as regularly reviewing procedures and company protocols.

Ensuring that the work environment is properly controlled and managed is essential for providing safe, effective, and high-quality services to clients while safeguarding the health and well-being of all staff involved in the procedures.

4. Prevention of Adverse Skin Reactions

Preventing adverse skin reactions is a crucial aspect of microblading, dermopigmentation, and eyebrow permanent makeup practices. These procedures involve applying pigments to the skin, which can lead to various unwanted reactions if not managed properly.

To prevent adverse skin reactions, it is essential to strictly follow best practices in hygiene and safety throughout all stages of the procedures. This includes using personal protective equipment (PPE), sterilizing tools, and controlling the work environment to minimize the risk of bacterial or viral contamination.

Additionally, a thorough evaluation of the client's skin before beginning any procedure is crucial. This can help identify any pre-existing skin conditions, allergies, or sensitivities that might increase the risk of adverse reactions. If necessary, the client should be advised to consult a dermatologist before proceeding with the treatment.

During the procedure itself, it is important to use high-quality, safe pigments that have been tested to minimize the risk of skin irritation or allergies. Furthermore, it is advisable to always perform a patch test on a small area of the skin before proceeding with the full pigment application, especially if the client has a history of skin sensitivity.

After the procedure, providing the client with detailed post-treatment care instructions is essential. This may include applying moisturizers or other recommended products to reduce irritation and promote quick and safe healing.

Finally, it is important to closely monitor the client for any signs of adverse skin reactions in the weeks following the procedure. If symptoms such as redness, swelling, itching, or excessive pain occur, the client should be advised to consult a physician or dermatologist immediately to assess the situation.

Taking precautions to prevent adverse skin reactions is essential for ensuring client safety and well-being and for maintaining high professional standards in microblading, dermopigmentation, and eyebrow permanent makeup practices.

5. Emergency Management During Procedures

Managing emergencies during microblading, dermopigmentation, and eyebrow permanent makeup procedures requires proper preparation and a quick, effective response in critical situations. While such situations are rare, being ready to handle them appropriately is essential for ensuring client safety and maintaining high professional standards.

One of the main emergencies during these procedures is hypotension, which can occur due to pain, stress, or an allergic reaction from the client. In the case of hypotension, it is important to immediately stop the procedure and position the client lying down with their legs elevated to promote blood flow to the brain. Administering fluids and sugars is also advisable to help raise blood pressure.

Another common emergency is hypoglycemia, which may occur if the client has not eaten sufficiently before the procedure or if they are sensitive to stress. In this case, it is important to provide the client with sugary foods or drinks to quickly raise their blood sugar levels and prevent any complications.

Additionally, being prepared to handle sudden allergic reactions to the pigments used during the procedure is crucial. If the client shows signs of an allergy, such as redness, swelling, or intense itching, it is essential to immediately stop the procedure and administer antihistamines or other emergency measures to relieve the symptoms.

In the event of more severe complications, such as bleeding or infections, having a well-stocked first aid kit and knowing how to use it correctly is vital. Prompt application of sterile dressings and consulting a physician are crucial for effectively managing such emergencies and preventing serious consequences for the client.

Finally, it is important to remain calm and act decisively in emergency situations during procedures. A quick and confident response can make the difference between a positive experience and a serious incident for the client. Therefore, regular training in emergency procedures and keeping safety and emergency management skills up-to-date is highly recommended.

XVI. Marketing and Promotion of Microblading and Dermopigmentation Services

1. Online Marketing Strategies

Online marketing strategies are crucial for successfully promoting microblading and dermopigmentation services. In an increasingly digital world, leveraging the web's potential is essential for reaching your target audience and boosting your business's visibility. Among the various strategies available, one of the most effective is developing a solid and consistent online presence across different digital channels.

Firstly, a well-designed website serves as the foundation of any online marketing strategy. The site should be user-friendly, easy to navigate, and optimized for search engines (SEO) to ensure good visibility in search results. It's important to include detailed information about the services offered, pricing, testimonials from satisfied clients, and any current promotions. Additionally, integrating an online booking system is advisable, allowing potential clients to conveniently schedule appointments directly from the site.

Alongside the website, maintaining an active and engaging presence on major social media platforms such as Facebook, Instagram, and Pinterest is essential. These channels offer a unique opportunity to share photos of results, video tutorials, practical tips, and more. Social media also allows for direct interaction with the audience, answering questions, managing reviews, and building a community around your brand.

In addition to managing social media channels, considering online advertising as a tool to reach a broader and more targeted audience is important. Advertising platforms like Google Ads and Facebook Ads allow for the creation of targeted ads based on demographic criteria, interests, and online behaviors. This enables you to reach potential clients who might be interested in your services, thereby increasing the chances of conversion.

Finally, implementing a content marketing strategy is useful by regularly producing relevant and informative content that engages your target audience. This content can include blog articles, practical guides, video tutorials, and more. Providing added value through content helps build trust with the audience and positions you as an authority in the field.

In summary, online marketing strategies offer a wide range of opportunities to promote microblading and dermopigmentation services, reach a broader audience, and enhance business success. However, it's important to carefully plan your online activities, monitor results, and adjust the strategy accordingly to maximize return on investment.

2. Collaborations with Influencers and Industry Professionals

Collaborating with influencers and industry professionals represents a strategic opportunity to enhance the visibility and credibility of your microblading and dermopigmentation business. Influencers, individuals with a significant following on social media and within the beauty sector, can have a substantial impact on brand perception and the ability to reach new clients.

The key to a successful collaboration with influencers is to identify those whose audience aligns with your ideal client base. This can be done by carefully analyzing their followers, the type of content they produce, and their reputation within the industry. Once the most suitable influencers are identified, collaboration can be initiated through various methods.

One common form of collaboration is providing free products or services to influencers in exchange for reviews or sponsored posts. This approach allows your brand to be introduced to a broader audience through the influencer's communication channel. It's important to establish clear agreements and expectations regarding the type of content and messaging to ensure an accurate and positive representation of your brand.

In addition to influencers, collaborating with other industry professionals can be equally advantageous. For example, partnering with estheticians, beauty salons, or dermatologists can help you reach new clients through an already established network of trusted clientele. This can be achieved through promotional partnerships, mutual referrals, or collaborative events.

Furthermore, participating in industry fairs, beauty events, or workshops can offer a unique opportunity to network with other professionals and promote your services. During these events, you can establish meaningful connections, share knowledge, and showcase your work through live demonstrations or presentations.

Lastly, it's important to maintain an authentic and genuine approach in collaborations with influencers and industry professionals. Transparency and integrity are crucial for building lasting and positive relationships with the audience and the professional community. Partnering with individuals who share your brand's values and vision can help ensure a successful and mutually beneficial long-term partnership.

3. Using Social Media to Promote Services

Utilizing social media is a crucial element for effectively and strategically promoting microblading and dermopigmentation services. Platforms like Instagram, Facebook, and TikTok offer a wide range of tools and features that allow you to reach a broad audience of potential clients and create an authentic and engaging brand image.

An effective social media strategy starts with creating high-quality, relevant content for your target audience. This can include photos and videos of treatment results, tutorials on specific techniques, behind-the-scenes glimpses of your work process, and testimonials from satisfied clients. It's important to maintain a balanced mix of informational, educational, and entertaining content to engage and retain audience attention over the long term.

Moreover, it is crucial to use the targeting and segmentation features offered by social media platforms to reach users most interested in your services. This can be achieved through targeted ads based on interests, demographics, and online behaviors. Additionally, using relevant and local hashtags can help increase the visibility of your content and attract potential local clients.

In addition to posting organic content, using paid advertising can be an effective way to expand the reach and engagement of your messages. Social media platforms offer various advertising options, including carousel ads, promotional videos, and sponsored story posts. These can be used to promote special offers, salon events, or to raise awareness about your brand.

Finally, it is important to maintain active interaction with your audience on social media by responding to comments, questions, and messages in a timely and courteous manner. This helps to build trust and authenticity with potential clients and keeps your brand top of mind over time.

4. Industry Events and Trade Shows: Promotional Opportunities

Participating in industry events and trade shows presents a unique opportunity to promote microblading and dermopigmentation services, meet new clients, and establish connections with other industry professionals. These events provide a platform to showcase your services tangibly, allowing potential clients to see the results firsthand and interact directly with salon staff.

Before attending an event or trade show, it is important to plan your presence carefully. This includes creating an attractive and professional booth or stand, with well-designed and informative promotional materials such as brochures, flyers, and samples of the products used in your salon. Additionally, adopting a proactive approach in engaging with booth visitors is essential—provide detailed information about your services, answer questions, and offer free consultations or special discounts for those who book during the event.

During the event, being present and visible is crucial. Actively participate in live demonstrations, workshops, and relevant industry conferences. This not only helps in promoting your services but also allows you to learn new techniques, trends, and best practices from other industry professionals.

Furthermore, you can leverage industry events and trade shows to form partnerships and collaborations with other professionals, such as estheticians, makeup artists, and hairstylists. These collaborations can lead to positive synergies and increased brand visibility through shared clientele and cross-promotion on respective marketing channels.

Finally, it is important to evaluate the effectiveness of participating in events and trade shows by monitoring key metrics such as the number of contacts generated, bookings made during the event, and overall return on investment. This information can be used to optimize future marketing and promotional strategies and to identify new growth and development opportunities for your business.

XVII. Equipment Management and Material Procurement

1. Equipment Selection: Choosing the Right Tool for Each Procedure

Selecting the right equipment is crucial for ensuring the success and safety of every microblading, dermopigmentation, and eyebrow permanent makeup procedure.

Each tool used in these practices must be carefully chosen, taking into account several factors that affect the effectiveness and precision of the work performed.

First and foremost, it is essential to evaluate the quality and reputation of the manufacturer, opting for reliable and well-known brands in the industry. The durability and reliability of the tools are crucial for ensuring consistent results over time and for avoiding complications during sessions.

Additionally, it is important to consider the specific needs of the professional and the characteristics of each procedure. For example, in microblading, it may be preferable to use thinner, more precise blades to create defined and natural lines, while in dermopigmentation, more robust and versatile tools might be needed to work on different skin types.

Equipment selection must also adhere to current regulations and guidelines in the permanent cosmetics industry, ensuring compliance with hygiene and safety standards to protect both the client's and the professional's health.

Finally, staying updated on new technologies and innovations in tools and equipment is vital for offering the best possible service to clients and remaining competitive in the market.

Choosing the right tool for each procedure is a fundamental step in ensuring high-quality results and meeting clients' expectations, contributing to the success and reputation of the professional in the fields of microblading, dermopigmentation, and eyebrow permanent makeup.

2. Maintenance and Cleaning of Equipment: Ensuring Safety and Longevity

Maintenance and cleaning of equipment are essential steps for ensuring the safety and longevity of the tools used in microblading, dermopigmentation, and eyebrow permanent makeup procedures.

Before each use, it is crucial to check that the tools are intact and free from damage, inspecting for any signs of wear or damaged parts that could compromise the effectiveness of the work and pose a risk to the client's health.

During and after each session, it is important to thoroughly clean the tools with disinfectants specifically designed for medical devices, capable of eliminating bacteria, viruses, and other pathogens that could contaminate the skin and cause infections.

Additionally, it is advisable to follow the manufacturer's guidelines and recommendations for proper maintenance of the tools, which may include tasks such as lubrication, sharpening, or replacing worn parts.

To ensure maximum safety and hygiene, it is important to dedicate a clean and well-organized space for storing the tools, avoiding contact with other surfaces or materials that could contaminate them.

Finally, it is important to keep track of expiration dates and recommended periodic checks from the manufacturer to ensure that the tools are always in optimal condition and compliant with current regulations in the permanent cosmetics industry.

Proper maintenance and cleaning of equipment are fundamental for ensuring client safety and the durability of tools used in microblading, dermopigmentation, and eyebrow permanent makeup practices, contributing to the success and reputation of the professional in the field.

3. Sourcing Materials: Strategies for Obtaining Quality Products

Sourcing materials is a crucial phase in ensuring the quality and effectiveness of services in microblading, dermopigmentation, and eyebrow permanent makeup. To obtain high-quality products, it is essential to follow specific strategies.

First, it is advisable to select reliable and reputable suppliers within the permanent cosmetics industry who offer certified products that comply with current regulations. Choosing established and trusted suppliers reduces the risk of acquiring counterfeit or substandard materials, ensuring both safety and effectiveness in the services provided.

Second, careful attention should be paid to the selection of individual products, evaluating characteristics such as composition, pigmentation, and longevity. Opting for high-quality materials and safe formulations is vital for achieving excellent results and meeting client expectations.

Another useful strategy is to consider the specific needs of your studio or salon and your clients, choosing materials and products that suit various skin types, aesthetic preferences, and individual requirements. Tailoring your material sourcing to your specific needs helps optimize work efficiency and deliver a customized service for each client.

Additionally, it is advisable to stay up-to-date with the latest innovations and trends in the permanent cosmetics industry by participating in trade shows, events, and specialized training courses. This allows you to discover new products, techniques, and methodologies, enhancing your professional knowledge and improving the quality of the services you offer.

Finally, attention should also be given to the cost-to-quality ratio of the materials purchased, carefully assessing the unit cost relative to the quality and reliability of the product. Finding a balance between quality and economic value helps optimize the budget and maximize the value of investments in your studio or salon.

4. Quality Control: Verification and Testing of Purchased Materials

Quality control of purchased materials is a crucial step in ensuring optimal performance and safety in microblading, dermopigmentation, and eyebrow permanent makeup treatments. Before using any product, it is essential to conduct thorough verification and testing of its characteristics and performance.

The first step involves carefully examining the product's packaging and labeling, ensuring that it includes all necessary information, such as expiration dates, ingredients, usage instructions, and safety warnings. Ensuring that the packaging is intact and free from signs of damage or tampering is crucial for verifying the product's authenticity and integrity.

Next, preliminary tests should be performed on a small area of skin, preferably on oneself or on willing models, to assess the product's compatibility with different skin types and minimize the risk of allergic reactions or skin irritations. This allows for the identification of any issues or incompatibilities before using the product on real clients.

During testing, it is important to evaluate the product's pigmentation, consistency, and longevity, checking whether it meets the expectations and specific needs of the treatment. If there are any doubts or concerns about the material's quality, it is advisable to contact the supplier for additional information or clarification.

In addition to preliminary tests, it is beneficial to maintain a detailed record of all materials purchased and used, noting any observations, client feedback, and results obtained during treatments. This helps monitor the effectiveness and reliability of products over time and make any necessary adjustments or improvements to your professional practice.

In conclusion, quality control of purchased materials is an ongoing and essential process for ensuring safety, effectiveness, and client satisfaction in microblading, dermopigmentation, and eyebrow permanent makeup treatments.

5. Workspace Organization: Optimizing for Maximum Efficiency

Organizing the workspace is crucial for ensuring maximum efficiency and comfort during microblading, dermopigmentation, and eyebrow permanent makeup sessions. A well-planned and optimized layout can make the difference between a smooth, productive workday and a frustrating, disorganized one.

Firstly, it's important to consider the physical arrangement of the tools and materials needed for the treatments. Ensuring that everything is easily accessible and logically arranged can reduce downtime and enhance workflow. For example, keeping pigments, blades, brushes, and other essential tools within reach allows the professional to focus fully on the task without interrupting the session to search for missing items.

Additionally, maintaining a clean, organized, and well-lit workspace is crucial. Regular cleaning of work surfaces and tools helps prevent cross-contamination and ensures a safe and hygienic environment for the client. Adequate lighting is essential for performing precise and accurate treatments, so ensuring a well-positioned and sufficient light source is fundamental.

Beyond the physical arrangement of tools, considering the ergonomics of the workspace is also important. Ensuring that the client is comfortably positioned and that the professional maintains proper posture during the treatment can help prevent long-term fatigue and musculoskeletal injuries.

Finally, having an organized system for managing client documentation and information, such as consultation forms, consent forms, and treatment records, is beneficial. Keeping these records easily accessible and up-to-date facilitates communication with clients and ensures efficient management of administrative tasks.

In summary, effective workspace organization is essential for maximizing efficiency and ensuring client safety and satisfaction during microblading, dermopigmentation, and eyebrow permanent makeup treatments.

6. Storage and Preservation: Maintaining Material Integrity Over Time

Storing and preserving materials are crucial steps in maintaining the integrity of the tools and products used in microblading, dermopigmentation, and eyebrow permanent makeup over the long term. A proper storage system not only protects tools from wear and contamination but also ensures the safety and effectiveness of the treatments.

Firstly, it's important to choose a storage area that is clean, dry, and well-ventilated. Excessive temperatures and humidity can compromise material quality, so it's advisable to avoid places subject to temperature fluctuations or extreme climatic conditions. Cabinets or shelves used for storage should be sturdy and stable to prevent accidental falls or damage to the tools.

Another important consideration is the organization and categorization of tools and materials to facilitate quick retrieval and access when needed. For instance, you might organize tools by category (e.g., blades, pigments, brushes) or by frequency of use. Using clear containers or clear labels can help easily identify the contents of each container and avoid confusion.

Additionally, it is advisable to keep tools and products well-protected from dust, dirt, and physical damage. Use protective cases or specific containers for delicate tools and package products carefully to protect them during transport or long-term storage. Ensuring that tools are properly cleaned and sterilized before storage can help prevent contamination and maintain tools in optimal condition.

Finally, it is important to track product expiration dates and materials to avoid using expired or deteriorated items. Keeping a log of purchases and expiration dates can help plan future acquisitions and ensure that tools and products are always fresh and usable.

In conclusion, proper storage and preservation are essential for maintaining the integrity of materials used in microblading, dermopigmentation, and eyebrow permanent makeup over the long term, ensuring safety, effectiveness, and client satisfaction.

7. Inventory Monitoring: Avoiding Stockouts and Ensuring Operational Continuity

Inventory monitoring is a crucial aspect of managing equipment and material procurement in the context of microblading, dermopigmentation, and eyebrow permanent makeup. Avoiding stockouts is essential for ensuring operational continuity and customer satisfaction. For this reason, adopting an accurate and systematic inventory monitoring system is advisable.

Firstly, it's important to establish a detailed list of all the tools, products, and materials needed for various procedures. This may include microblading blades, pigments, needles, brushes, disinfectant wipes, masks, and more. Once the list is compiled, it is useful to define optimal quantities of each item to keep in stock based on usage frequency and business needs.

Next, it is advisable to track inventory using a regular inventory system. This can be done manually through paper records or by using inventory management software. The key is to ensure that the chosen system is accurate, user-friendly, and regularly updated to reflect stock variations.

In addition to monitoring quantities, it is also helpful to keep an eye on the quality of materials. For example, regularly checking the expiration dates of products ensures they remain usable and safe. Monitoring the quality of tools and materials can also help identify signs of wear or deterioration, allowing for timely replacement or repair.

Another important consideration is anticipating reordering needs. By proactively monitoring inventory, you can predict when new orders will be necessary and ensure that you always have what you need to operate without interruptions.

Finally, maintaining a close relationship with suppliers is advisable to ensure a reliable and timely supply chain. Regular communication with suppliers can help avoid delivery delays and address any issues that may arise during the procurement process.

In conclusion, inventory monitoring is essential for avoiding stockouts and ensuring operational continuity in microblading, dermopigmentation, and eyebrow permanent makeup. By adopting an accurate and systematic monitoring system, you can effectively manage inventory and ensure smooth business operations.

8. Sustainability and Waste Reduction: Eco-Friendly Practices for Managing Equipment and Materials

In the fields of microblading, dermopigmentation, and eyebrow permanent makeup, adopting sustainable practices and reducing waste is crucial for promoting an eco-friendly approach to managing equipment and materials. There are several strategies professionals can use to lessen the environmental impact of their work and contribute to the protection of our planet.

Firstly, a sustainable practice involves optimizing resource use by minimizing material waste. This can be achieved by employing efficient work techniques that maximize the use of tools and products while minimizing excessive consumption. For instance, avoiding the use of more product than necessary during procedures and reducing the number of tools used can help cut down on waste and conserve resources.

Secondly, it is important to choose eco-friendly materials and equipment whenever possible. This might include purchasing products made from recycled or biodegradable materials and using tools with a reduced environmental impact during production and disposal. Additionally, seeking suppliers who adopt sustainable practices and offer eco-friendly options can contribute to a more sustainable supply chain.

Another important practice is recycling and proper disposal of materials. Recycling packaging and product containers, as well as disposing of tools and equipment correctly at the end of their useful life, can help reduce the environmental impact of professional activities. Additionally, exploring recycling opportunities or donating unused equipment can help reduce waste and give materials a second life.

Finally, educating clients about the importance of sustainability and encouraging them to make eco-friendly choices is essential. This can be done by providing information about the sustainable products and practices used in the studio and promoting the adoption of sustainable habits among clients. For example, encouraging clients to recycle product packaging and choose eco-friendly treatments can help spread environmental awareness and foster more sustainable behaviors.

In conclusion, adopting sustainable practices and reducing waste is fundamental for promoting an eco-friendly approach to managing equipment and materials in microblading, dermopigmentation, and eyebrow permanent makeup. Choosing eco-friendly materials, optimizing resource use, recycling, and educating clients are just a few of the strategies professionals can implement to minimize their environmental impact and contribute to the protection of our planet.

XVIII. Legal and Regulatory Aspects of Microblading and Dermopigmentation Practice

1. Legislation on Cosmetic Practices: Regulations and Legal Requirements

Legislation on cosmetic practices is a fundamental pillar in ensuring the safety and quality of microblading and dermopigmentation services. Regulations and legal requirements vary from country to country and are often subject to frequent updates to keep pace with technological advancements and new discoveries in the cosmetic field. These regulations are designed to protect client health and well-being, as well as to establish standards of competence and professionalism for industry practitioners.

A primary aspect of cosmetic practice legislation concerns the registration and authorization of products used during microblading and dermopigmentation treatments. Regulatory bodies may require that pigments and other materials meet specific safety and quality standards. This can include verifying the chemical composition of pigments, their stability, and their compliance with cosmetic product safety regulations.

Additionally, legislation usually sets out training and certification requirements for practitioners who wish to perform microblading and dermopigmentation. These requirements may involve completing specific training courses, acquiring practical skills under the supervision of qualified professionals, and obtaining certifications recognized by the relevant authorities. Continuing education may also be required to maintain a license or professional certification.

Other regulatory aspects include guidelines on hygiene and safety during treatments, such as practices for disinfecting and sterilizing tools and equipment, as well as procedures for managing biological and chemical waste. These standards are designed to prevent the spread of infections and ensure a safe environment for both clients and practitioners.

Moreover, legislation may also regulate advertising and promotional practices in the microblading and dermopigmentation sector, establishing rules and restrictions on the use of efficacy claims, client testimonials, and before-and-after images. This aims to ensure that information provided to potential clients is accurate and not misleading.

Finally, civil and criminal liability laws may define the legal consequences of negligent or harmful professional practices. Practitioners may be required to obtain specific insurance policies to protect themselves from potential legal disputes and claims for damages from clients.

In summary, legislation on cosmetic practices plays a crucial role in ensuring the safety, effectiveness, and integrity of microblading and dermopigmentation procedures, establishing rules and regulations that guide industry practitioners and protect client rights and well-being.

2. Training and Certification Requirements for Industry Professionals

Training and certification requirements for professionals in the microblading and dermopigmentation fields are essential to ensure that practitioners are adequately prepared and competent to provide safe and effective services to their clients. These requirements vary depending on the regulations in each country or region and are often subject to periodic updates to reflect the latest standards and best practices in the cosmetic industry.

Regulatory authorities may establish specific criteria that practitioners must meet before obtaining the necessary license or certification to legally perform microblading and dermopigmentation. This can include participation in approved training courses covering topics such as skin anatomy, color theory, pigment application techniques, hygiene standards, and risk management.

In some cases, practitioners may be required to demonstrate their skills through theoretical and practical exams to assess their knowledge and abilities. These exams may be conducted by accredited organizations or training institutions recognized by the relevant authorities.

Continuing education is often a requirement to maintain a license or professional certification in the microblading and dermopigmentation fields. Practitioners may be required to attend periodic refresher courses to stay up-to-date with new technologies, industry trends, and innovations in procedures and materials.

Additionally, industry professionals may choose to pursue advanced or specialized certifications to demonstrate specific expertise in particular techniques or areas of interest, such as eyebrow microblading, lip or scalp dermopigmentation, or scar correction.

The goal of training and certification requirements is to ensure that industry practitioners possess the knowledge, skills, and capabilities needed to offer safe, effective, and high-quality treatments to their clients, minimizing the risk of complications or damage.

3. Legal and Insurance Responsibilities for Microblading and Dermopigmentation Practitioners

Legal and insurance responsibilities are crucial aspects for practitioners in the microblading and dermopigmentation fields, providing essential protection for both themselves and their clients. Being aware of legal and insurance implications is fundamental for managing potential risks and safeguarding the integrity of their business.

Firstly, practitioners must understand the laws and regulations applicable in their country or region that govern the practice of microblading and dermopigmentation. These laws may address issues such as the safety of products used, hygiene standards, client age restrictions, and other legal provisions affecting professional practice.

A proper understanding of legal responsibilities can help practitioners avoid potential legal disputes and manage client complaints effectively and efficiently. This includes being aware of client rights, informed consent procedures, and refund or compensation policies in cases of dissatisfaction or issues during treatment.

Additionally, it is essential for practitioners to have adequate insurance coverage to protect themselves from potential claims for physical damage, complications, or client dissatisfaction. Insurance policies specific to the microblading and dermopigmentation industry can cover a wide range of risks, including incidents during treatment, allergic reactions to pigments, and other unforeseen events that may occur during professional practice.

Insurance policies can vary based on the coverage offered, so it is important for practitioners to carefully assess their insurance needs and choose a policy that provides comprehensive and adequate protection for their business. This may include coverage for professional liability, property damage, theft or damage to equipment, and other contingencies that could affect business continuity and reputation.

Ultimately, legal and insurance responsibilities are a fundamental component of professional practice in the microblading and dermopigmentation sector. Practitioners must be diligently informed about applicable laws and regulations and ensure they have comprehensive insurance coverage to protect themselves, their clients, and their business from potential risks and legal disputes.

4. Health and Safety Regulations to Ensure Client Safety

Health and safety regulations are a fundamental pillar of microblading and dermopigmentation practices, ensuring the safety and well-being of clients during treatments. These regulations are designed to prevent the transmission of infections and diseases and to maintain a clean and safe working environment for both practitioners and clients.

Firstly, practitioners must strictly adhere to hygiene guidelines established by relevant health authorities in their country or region. These guidelines may include provisions for the disinfection and sterilization of equipment, personal hygiene of practitioners, management of biological and chemical waste, and other practices that reduce the risk of cross-contamination and infection spread.

Practitioners should implement rigorous procedures for cleaning and disinfecting all tools and surfaces used during treatments, including microblades, dermopigmentation needles, pigment containers, brushes, and other accessories. It is crucial to use approved disinfectants and meticulously follow instructions to ensure the effectiveness of the sterilization process.

Moreover, practitioners need to adopt proper hygiene practices during treatments, such as thoroughly washing hands with soap and water before and after each client, wearing disposable gloves during the treatment, and using face masks and head coverings to minimize the risk of microbial contamination.

In addition to hygiene regulations, it is important for practitioners to maintain a clean and organized work environment. This includes regularly cleaning work surfaces, replacing table linens and disposable covers between clients, and properly managing waste.

Finally, practitioners should be prepared to handle emergency situations and provide a safe environment for clients during treatments. This may involve training in first aid procedures, having well-stocked first aid kits available, and knowing how to manage any allergic reactions or complications that may arise during treatments.

In conclusion, health and safety regulations are an essential component of microblading and dermopigmentation practices. Practitioners must adopt stringent hygiene practices and comply with guidelines established by health authorities to ensure client safety and the success of their business.

5. Documentation and Informed Consent: Role and Importance in Aesthetic Treatments

Documentation and informed consent play a crucial role in microblading and dermopigmentation practices, serving as essential tools to inform clients about the proposed treatments, associated risks, and expected outcomes, as well as to protect practitioners from potential legal disputes.

Before performing any aesthetic treatment, practitioners should provide clients with comprehensive and detailed documentation describing the procedure, its implications, and potential risks. This documentation should include information about the materials used, possible side effects, contraindications, as well as post-treatment care instructions for optimal healing. Additionally, it should outline the expected results, including healing times and any potential need for touch-ups.

Informed consent is a document signed by the client indicating that they have received all necessary information about the treatment and understand the associated risks and benefits. Signing the informed consent form signifies that the client agrees to undergo the treatment knowingly and voluntarily, releasing the practitioner from legal liability in the event of any complications.

In addition to informed consent, practitioners are advised to maintain detailed records of each treatment performed, including client details, procedures carried out, materials used, and any other relevant information. This documentation can be useful for legal purposes, monitoring client progress over time, and ensuring better care for touch-ups or subsequent treatments.

Therefore, documentation and informed consent are indispensable tools for ensuring professional and ethical practices in the field of microblading and dermopigmentation. They provide a solid foundation for communication between practitioner and client, ensuring that both parties are fully informed and aware of the risks and benefits of aesthetic treatments.

XIX. Troubleshooting and Managing Challenges During Procedures

1. Identifying Issues During Procedures

During microblading, dermopigmentation, and eyebrow permanent makeup procedures, it is crucial to be prepared to address any issues that may arise during the treatment. Timely identification of these problems is essential to ensure client safety and achieve optimal results.

One of the most common issues that may occur is related to the shape and symmetry of the eyebrows. Discrepancies in the desired shape or symmetry between the two eyebrows may arise while mapping out guidelines for microblading or applying pigment for dermopigmentation. This could be due to various factors, including errors in facial analysis, measurement discrepancies, or simply the natural asymmetry of the human face. Advanced skills in facial analysis and eyebrow design are necessary to promptly identify and address these issues.

Additionally, allergic reactions to the pigment used or excessive bleeding might occur during the treatment. These are just a few examples of problems that can arise during microblading and dermopigmentation procedures. An experienced professional must be able to quickly identify such situations and take appropriate measures to manage them in the safest and most effective way possible.

Besides issues related to eyebrow shape and symmetry, it is important to be aware of potential risks associated with the treatment itself. For instance, bacterial or viral infections can occur if equipment is not properly sterilized or if hygienic practices are not diligently followed. Knowledge of hygiene standards and adherence to proper procedures are crucial for preventing such risks.

During the procedure, the client might also experience pain or discomfort. Effective communication with the client is essential to ensure their comfort and satisfaction. This may include applying topical anesthetics before the treatment or adjusting pressure during microblading to minimize discomfort.

Lastly, post-treatment healing issues, such as pigment rejection or complications like hyperpigmentation or infection, can occur. Proper follow-up with the client and providing detailed post-treatment care instructions can help mitigate these risks and ensure satisfactory results.

In conclusion, timely identification of issues during microblading and dermopigmentation procedures is crucial for ensuring client safety and achieving optimal results. An experienced professional must be capable of addressing a wide range of challenges effectively and safely, providing high-quality and satisfactory treatment for the client.

2. Real-Time Problem-Solving Strategies

During microblading and dermopigmentation procedures, having effective strategies for addressing problems as they arise in real-time is crucial. These strategies require a combination of technical skills, practical experience, and quick decision-making to ensure that the treatment proceeds smoothly and the client is satisfied with the results.

One of the most important strategies is to remain calm and maintain a professional attitude even in critical situations. Staying calm helps reduce stress and anxiety for both the professional and the client, creating a more comfortable environment conducive to the treatment process. Additionally, a composed professional is more likely to make rational decisions and take appropriate actions to resolve issues effectively.

In addition to staying calm, it is essential to be flexible and adaptable to the client's changing needs and the various challenges that may arise during the treatment. This may involve adjusting the treatment plan based on the client's preferences or the skin's response to the pigment. Being able to quickly adapt to changing circumstances is crucial for achieving optimal results and client satisfaction.

Another important strategy is to communicate openly and clearly with the client throughout the treatment process. Explaining the steps of the treatment, answering questions, and providing updates on the treatment's progress helps keep the client informed and engaged in the decision-making process. Moreover, effective communication can help alleviate the client's anxiety and discomfort, contributing to a more positive overall experience.

In some cases, it may be necessary to modify the technique or treatment method to address a specific problem. For example, if excessive bleeding occurs during the treatment, it might be necessary to temporarily stop the procedure to apply more pressure or use hemostatic products to stop the bleeding. Quickly assessing the situation and taking appropriate measures is crucial for ensuring client safety and treatment success.

Finally, it is important to keep a record of the problems encountered during the treatment and the strategies used to resolve them. Maintaining a detailed log of these incidents can provide valuable insights for improving future practices and preventing similar issues. Additionally, it can be useful for training purposes and ensuring compliance with regulations and legal requirements.

In summary, real-time problem-solving strategies during microblading and dermopigmentation procedures are essential for ensuring treatment success and client satisfaction. Staying calm, being flexible, communicating effectively, taking appropriate measures, and keeping track of encountered issues are all key elements of these strategies, helping manage challenges with confidence and efficiency.

3. Managing Post-Treatment Complications

Managing post-treatment complications is a crucial aspect of microblading and dermopigmentation practice, as adverse reactions or unforeseen problems can occur after the treatment is completed. It is essential to be prepared to address these situations promptly and effectively to ensure client safety and satisfaction.

One of the most common post-treatment complications involves skin reactions, such as redness, swelling, or itching, which may manifest after the procedure. These reactions can be caused by various factors, including the application of pigments incompatible with the client's skin, an allergic reaction to the materials used, or inadequate hygiene during the treatment. To manage these complications, it is vital to provide the client with detailed aftercare instructions and recommend any topical products or treatments that may help alleviate the symptoms. Additionally, closely monitoring the client's skin condition and offering further advice and support if necessary is important.

Another potential post-treatment complication is irregular or unwanted pigmentation. This might appear as dark or light spots on the skin, overly intense or faded pigment, or even the formation of uneven lines or smudges. Addressing these issues requires a careful assessment to determine the underlying cause. In some cases, corrective treatments may be needed to remove or adjust the undesired pigment. It is important to communicate openly with the client about available options and set realistic expectations for corrective treatment outcomes.

Other post-treatment complications may include infections in the treated area, bleeding, and the formation of scabs or scars. These issues require immediate attention and may necessitate additional medical care. Being able to recognize the signs of these complications and act swiftly to minimize the risk of severe or permanent issues is crucial. Moreover, it is important to document any post-treatment complications and the measures taken to address them, ensuring compliance with regulations and legal requirements while protecting professional reputation and liability.

In summary, managing post-treatment complications requires a combination of technical skills, practical experience, and quick decision-making. Being prepared to handle a range of problems that may arise after the treatment and providing the client with comprehensive support and personalized guidance is essential for addressing complications safely and effectively.

4. Effective Communication with Clients During Issues

Effective communication with clients during issues that may arise in microblading and dermopigmentation procedures plays a crucial role in ensuring transparency, trust, and optimal management of challenging situations. It is important to establish open and clear communication from the start of the treatment, providing clients with detailed information about potential complications and the steps to follow if problems arise.

When issues occur during the procedure or in the post-treatment period, maintaining calm and reassuring communication with the client is essential. Listening attentively to the client's concerns and responding empathetically and professionally can help reduce anxiety and build a foundation of mutual trust. Explaining the nature of the problem, possible causes, and available options for resolution is crucial for actively involving the client in the decision-making process and ensuring they feel engaged in their care journey.

In communication with clients during issues, it is important to use clear and accessible language, avoiding overly complex technical terms that may confuse or alarm the client. Using understandable examples and analogies can help make information more accessible and facilitate the client's comprehension.

Additionally, providing the client with a realistic estimate of problem resolution times and potential impacts on the final treatment outcome is important. This helps the client fully understand the situation and manage their expectations regarding the expected results.

Finally, accurately documenting all communications with the client regarding issues and the actions taken to address them is essential. This not only helps maintain a detailed record of the issue management process but can also be valuable from a legal perspective in case of disputes or client complaints.

In summary, effective communication with clients during issues is a key aspect of microblading and dermopigmentation practice. Providing clear information, actively listening to client concerns, and involving them in the decision-making process are fundamental for managing difficult situations professionally and empathetically.

5. Continuous Improvement of Work Processes

Continuous improvement of work processes is a fundamental pillar for ensuring the quality, efficiency, and safety of microblading and dermopigmentation procedures. This approach is based on the idea of constantly identifying areas for optimization and implementing improvements to ensure increasingly higher standards in professional practice.

To initiate a process of continuous improvement, it is essential to regularly conduct detailed assessments of current work procedures, identifying strengths, weaknesses, and development opportunities. This analysis can be carried out through periodic internal reviews, involving the staff engaged in the procedures and collecting feedback from clients to understand their experiences and expectations.

Once areas for improvement have been identified, it is important to develop and implement targeted action plans to address issues and optimize existing processes. These plans should be based on specific, measurable objectives, with clear guidelines on how to achieve these goals and a timeline for monitoring progress over time.

During the implementation of improvements, actively involving the staff involved in the procedures is crucial, providing training and adequate support to ensure a smooth transition and full adherence to new work practices. Additionally, maintaining a flexible and adaptable approach is important, allowing for the review and updating of processes based on evolving industry needs and received feedback.

Another key element of continuous improvement of work processes is the collection and analysis of performance and outcome data. This may include metrics such as the time taken to complete a procedure, the success rate of treatments, client satisfaction levels, and more. Using this information, trends can be identified, potential issues pinpointed, and the impact of implemented improvements evaluated.

In conclusion, continuous improvement of work processes is a dynamic and proactive approach that allows microblading and dermopigmentation professionals to maintain high standards of quality, efficiency, and safety in their practice. By fostering a culture of ongoing learning and development, it is possible to ensure increasingly better service for clients and remain competitive in an ever-evolving market.

XX. Professional Development and Skill Advancement in Microblading and Permanent Makeup

1. Advanced Training Programs and Specializations

Advanced training programs and specializations represent a crucial step forward in professional development in the field of microblading and permanent makeup.

These programs provide professionals with the opportunity to deepen their knowledge, acquire specialized skills, and stay current with the latest trends and innovations in the industry.

Advanced training can cover a wide range of topics, including more complex technical approaches, new methodologies, management of challenging cases, and much more.

Specialization courses are designed to provide participants with in-depth, practical knowledge on specific aspects of microblading and permanent makcup, allowing them to stand out in the market and meet the increasingly sophisticated needs of their clientele.

These programs may be offered by accredited training institutes, specialized beauty centers, or directly by experienced professionals in the field, and often include hands-on sessions, interactive workshops, and personalized mentoring.

Participating in advanced training programs and specializations is crucial for anyone aiming to achieve excellence in microblading and permanent makeup, as they provide the skills and knowledge necessary to tackle complex challenges and deliver high-quality results.

2. Continuing Education Courses and Hands-On Workshops

Continuing education courses and hands-on workshops provide a valuable opportunity for microblading and permanent makeup professionals to stay updated with the latest industry advancements and trends.

These courses are designed to give trained practitioners the chance to expand their skills, learn new techniques, and refine their existing abilities.

During hands-on workshops, participants can apply the knowledge they've gained by working on live models or realistic simulations. This type of training offers invaluable practical experience, allowing professionals to hone their techniques and receive direct feedback from experienced instructors.

Continuing education courses can cover a broad range of topics, including the latest eyebrow design trends, new application techniques, post-treatment complication management, and more.

Participating in continuing education courses and hands-on workshops is essential for staying competitive in the ever-evolving field of microblading and permanent makeup. It helps professionals keep their skills and knowledge aligned with best practices and the latest trends.

3. Advanced Microblading Techniques Mastery

Mastering advanced microblading techniques is a crucial step for professionals aiming to stand out in the industry and deliver high-quality, long-lasting results to their clients.

These advanced courses focus on specific aspects of microblading, such as designing eyebrows according to each client's unique facial features, using different blades and pigments to achieve personalized effects, and correcting any errors or imperfections.

Experienced instructors guide participants through practical exercises and detailed demonstrations, offering advice and tips to refine techniques and achieve flawless results.

Topics covered may also include managing complications during the healing process, creating three-dimensional effects for a more natural look, and applying innovative techniques for fuller and more defined eyebrows.

Participating in advanced microblading technique courses is especially beneficial for professionals who wish to elevate their skill level and provide superior, customized services to their clients.

These courses offer the opportunity to gain a deeper understanding of best practices and the latest innovations in microblading, enabling professionals to become leaders in the field and better meet their clients' needs.

4. Exploring New Technologies in Permanent Makeup

Exploring new technologies in permanent makeup represents a significant milestone in advancing professional skills within the industry. Technological innovations provide new opportunities to enhance the precision, efficiency, and overall results of dermopigmentation treatments.

Among the most promising new technologies are advanced digital pigmentation devices, which allow professionals to precisely control the depth and distribution of pigment on the skin. These devices feature sophisticated functionalities, such as pressure and speed control systems, which enable more defined and even lines.

Additionally, new technologies include the use of innovative pigments and materials that offer greater longevity and resistance over time. For example, microencapsulated pigments are better able to withstand degradation from sunlight and the skin's healing processes, ensuring more stable and long-lasting results.

Other developing technologies involve advanced imaging systems, such as digital skin mapping and augmented reality, which allow professionals to view the structure and texture of the skin in greater detail before performing the treatment.

Participating in workshops and training courses focused on new technologies in permanent makeup is essential for staying current with the latest industry developments and for acquiring the skills necessary to effectively use these innovative technologies.

Exploring new technologies in permanent makeup represents an investment in professional excellence and the ability to offer increasingly advanced and high-quality treatments to clients.

5. Certification Paths and Professional Recognition

Certification paths and professional recognition are crucial for practitioners in the microblading and permanent makeup industry, as they confirm the competence and quality of their work. These pathways offer practitioners the opportunity to acquire the necessary knowledge and skills to perform safe and effective treatments, as well as to stay updated on the latest trends and technologies in the field.

Certification courses cover a wide range of topics, including hygiene and safety, color theory, pigment application techniques, client management, and pre- and post-treatment consultation. Through practical and theoretical sessions, practitioners have the chance to learn and apply the skills needed to become qualified professionals in the industry.

Obtaining recognized certification is an important step in a microblading and permanent makeup practitioner's career, as it provides a valid testament to their skills and knowledge in the eyes of clients and potential employers. Recognized certifications are issued by accredited institutes and organizations in the cosmetic industry, ensuring high standards and compliance with current regulations.

Moreover, professional recognition offers practitioners the opportunity to stand out in the market and enhance their credibility and reputation. Certified professionals are often preferred by clients seeking high-quality and safe treatments, as certification is a sign of commitment to excellence and adherence to best practices in the industry.

Participating in certification programs and achieving professional recognition not only contributes to individual skill improvement but also to the growth and development of the entire microblading and permanent makeup sector. Qualified and well-trained practitioners help promote high standards of safety and quality in cosmetic treatments, ensuring client satisfaction and trust over the long term.

In conclusion, certification paths and professional recognition play a crucial role in ensuring the quality and safety of microblading and permanent makeup treatments, providing practitioners with the skills and credentials necessary to excel in the field.

Want one of our books for only $0.99? Here's how!

Hi there!
If you enjoyed this book, you can get your next title **for just $0.99**, choosing between:

- eBook
- PDF of a print book

Follow these simple steps:

1. Share your experience on the site where you purchased the book.

2. Send a screenshot **of your feedback**, showing the "Verified Purchase" label, to:
info.testicreativi@gmail.com

3. You'll receive a personal discount code to use in our online store, valid to get your next book **for only $0.99**.

Your opinion truly matters: every review helps us grow and allows new readers to discover our books.

Thank you so much for your time, and happy reading!

www.ingramcontent.com/pod-product-compliance
Lightning Source LLC
Chambersburg PA
CBHW071917210526
45479CB00002B/452